VERMONT COVERED BRIDGES

KINGSLEY BRIDGE • East Clarendon

VERMONT
COVERED BRIDGES

A Traveler's Guide

ERIC RIBACK

*Illustrated guide with maps and location
details to help you find more than 100
authentic covered bridges*

BELLA ✸ TERRA®

Bella Terra Publishing
P.O. Box 731
Rhinebeck, NY 12572
bellaterramaps.com

Book designed by Kate Winter
Illustrations by Peter M. Mason, except for Shoreham Railroad Bridge
© Gerald C. Hill
Maps by Kate Winter

Printed in the United States of America.
ISBN 978-1-888216-62-2

CONTENTS

LIST OF ILLUSTRATIONS viii
INTRODUCTION 1
BRIDGE TRUSS FRAMES 3
BRIDGE INDEX BY TOWN 4

THE BRIDGES

A.M. Foster Bridge 11
Arlington Bridge – *see West Arlington Bridge*
Baltimore Bridge 11
Bartonsville Bridge 12
Battleground Bridge 12
Bennington Falls Bridge – *see Paper Mill Bridge (Bennington)*
Best Bridge 13
Best Western Bridge 13
Big Eddy Bridge – *see Village Bridge*
Black Falls Bridge – *see Fuller Bridge*
Black River Bridge – *see Orne Bridge*
Blaisdell Bridge – *see Braley Bridge*
Bowers Bridge 14
Bradley Bridge – *see Miller's Run Bridge*
Braley Bridge 14
Brewster River Bridge – *see Grist Mill Bridge*
Bridge at the Green – *see West Arlington Bridge*
Brookdale Bridge 15
Brown Bridge 15
Brown's River Bridge 16
Brownsville Bridge – *see Bowers Bridge*
Burrington Bridge – *see Randall Bridge*
Burt Henry Bridge – *see Henry Bridge*

i

C.K. Smith Bridge – *see Gifford Bridge*

Cambridge Bridge – *see Shelburne Museum Bridge*

Cambridge Junction Bridge – *see Poland Bridge*

Canyon Bridge – *see Grist Mill Bridge*

Cedar Swamp Bridge – *see Salisbury Station Bridge*

Cemetery Bridge – *see Coburn Bridge*

Centre Bridge – *see Sanborn Bridge*

Chaffee Bridge – *see Red Bridge*

Chamberlin Bridge (Lyndon) – *see Chamberlin Mill Bridge*

Chamberlin Bridge 16

Chamberlin Mill Bridge 17

Chase Bridge – *see Schoolhouse Bridge*

Cheddar Bridge 17

Chiselville Bridge 18

Chubb Bridge – *see Fisher Railroad Bridge*

Church Street Bridge 18

Cilley Bridge 19

Coburn Bridge 19

Codding Hollow Bridge – *see Jaynes Bridge*

Columbia Bridge 21

Comstock Bridge 21

Cooley Bridge 22

Corgi Crossing Bridge 22

Cornish-Windsor Bridge 23

Cornwall-Salisbury Bridge – *see Salisbury Station Bridge*

Coventry Bridge – *see Orne Bridge*

Creamery Bridge (Brattleboro) 23

Creamery Bridge (Montgomery) – *see West Hill Bridge*

Crystal Springs Bridge – *see West Hill Bridge*

Degoosh Bridge – *see Scribner Bridge*

Depot Bridge 24

Depot Bridge (Rockingham) – *see Victorian Village Bridge*

Downers Bridge – *see Upper Falls Bridge*

Dummerston Bridge – *see West Dummerston Bridge*

East Fairfield Bridge 24

Emily's Bridge 25

Fairfax Bridge – *see Maple Street Bridge*

First Bridge – *see Station Bridge*

Fisher Railroad Bridge 25

Flint Bridge 27

Florence Station Bridge – *see Depot Bridge*

Frank Lewis Bridge 27

Fuller Bridge 28

Gates Farm Bridge 28

Gibou Road Bridge – *see Hectorville Bridge*

Gifford Bridge 29

Gold Brook Bridge – *see Emily's Bridge*

Goodnough Bridge – *see Gorham Bridge*

Gorham Bridge 29

Great Eddy Bridge – *see Village Bridge*

Green River Bridge 31

Greenbanks Hollow Bridge 31

Grist Mill Bridge 32

Guy Bridge – *see Moxley Bridge*

Hall Bridge 32

Halpin Bridge 33

Hammond Bridge 33

Harnois Bridge – *see Longley Bridge*

Hayward Bridge – *see Mill Bridge (Tunbridge)*

Head Bridge – *see Longley Bridge*

Hectorville Bridge 34

Henry Bridge 34

High Bridge – *see Halpin Bridge*

High Mowing Farm Bridge 35

Hitchcock-Cormier Bridge 35

Hollow Bridge – *see Brown Bridge*

Holmes Creek Bridge 36

Hopkins Bridge 36

iii

Howe Bridge...37
Hutchins Bridge..37
Hyde Bridge – *see Kingsbury Bridge*
Irasburg Bridge – *see Orne Bridge*
Island Pond Footbridge 39
Jaynes Bridge 39
Johnny Esau Footbridge 40
Johnson Bridge (Johnson) – *see Power House Bridge*
Johnson Bridge (Randolph) – *see Braley Bridge*
Kent's Corner Bridge...40
Kidder Hill Bridge 41
Kingsbury Bridge...41
Kingsley Bridge 42
Kissing Bridge (Waterville) – *see Jaynes Bridge*
Kissing Bridge (Jeffersonville) – *see Poland Bridge*
Lake Shore Bridge – *see Holmes Creek Bridge*
Larkin Bridge...42
Ledoux Hometown Footbridge 43
Lincoln Bridge..43
Lincoln Gap Bridge – *see Warren Bridge*
Locust Grove Bridge – *see Silk Bridge*
Longley Bridge...45
Lord's Creek Bridge...45
Lower Bridge – *see Quinlan Bridge*
Lower Cox Brook Bridge – *see Second Bridge*
Lumber Mill Bridge 46
MacMillan Bridge – *see Cheddar Bridge*
Maple Street Bridge 46
Martin Bridge 47
Martin's Mill Bridge 47
Martinsville Bridge – *see Martin's Mill Bridge*
Meat Market Bridge – *see Church Street Bridge*
Middle Bridge 48
Mill Bridge (Belvidere) – *see Lumber Mill Bridge*

Mill Bridge (Tunbridge)..48

Mill River Bridge – *see Kingsley Bridge*

Miller's Run Bridge...49

Montgomery Bridge 49

Morgan Bridge 51

Moseley Bridge..51

Mount Orne Bridge..52

Moxley Bridge 52

Mudget Bridge – *see Scribner Bridge*

Newell Bridge – *see Second Bridge*

Noble Bridge – *see Mill Bridge (Tunbridge)*

North Hartland Bridge – *see Willard Bridge*

Northfield Falls Bridge – *see Station Bridge*

Old Burrington Bridge – *see Randall Bridge*

Old Hollow Bridge – *see Spade Farm Bridge*

Orne Bridge...53

Orton Farm Bridge – *see Martin Bridge*

Osgood Bridge – *see Hall Bridge*

Paper Mill Bridge (Bennington)..53

Paper Mill Bridge (Middlebury) – *see Pulp Mill Bridge*

Paper Mill Village Bridge – *see Paper Mill Bridge (Bennington)*

Pine Brook Bridge..54

Poland Bridge...54

Post Office Bridge – *see Fuller Bridge*

Potter Bridge – *see Montgomery Bridge*

Power House Bridge 55

Pulp Mill Bridge...55

Quechee Bridge..57

Quinlan Bridge...57

Randall Bridge 58

Red Bridge..58

River Road Bridge..59

Roaring Branch Bridge – *see Chiselville Bridge*

Robbins Nest Bridge 59

Robinson Bridge – *see Silk Bridge*

Rutland Railroad Bridge – *see Shoreham Railroad Bridge*

Salisbury Station Bridge 60

Salmond Bridge 60

Sanborn Bridge 61

Sanderson Bridge 61

Sayres Bridge – *see Thetford Center Bridge*

School Bridge – *see River Road Bridge*

School House Bridge (Troy) – *see River Road Bridge*

School Street Bridge – *see Power House Bridge*

Schoolhouse Bridge.. 62

Scott Bridge (Jeffersonville) – *see Grist Mill Bridge*

Scott Bridge (Townshend) 62

Scribner Bridge 63

Second Bridge 63

Seguin Bridge.. 64

Shelburne Museum Bridge 64

Sherman Bridge – *see Quinlan Bridge*

Shoreham Railroad Bridge... 65

Silk Bridge 65

Slaughter House Bridge 67

Smith Bridge – *see Teago Bridge*

Snow Bridge.. 67

South Pomfret Bridge – *see Teago Bridge*

South Randolph Bridge – *see Kingsbury Bridge*

Spade Farm Bridge.. 68

Station Bridge.. 68

Station Bridge (Cambridge) – *see Poland Bridge*

Sterling Brook Bridge – *see Red Bridge*

Stony Brook Bridge – *see Moseley Bridge*

Stoughton Bridge – *see Titcomb Bridge*

Stowe Hollow Bridge – *see Emily's Bridge*

Stowe Walkway Bridge 69

Swallows Bridge – *see Best Bridge*

vi

Taftsville Bridge 69
Teago Bridge 70
Thetford Center Bridge 70
Third Bridge 71
Titcomb Bridge 71
Twin Bridge 72
Union Street Bridge – *see Middle Bridge*
Union Village Bridge 72
Upper Bridge – *see Seguin Bridge*
Upper Cox Brook Bridge – *see Third Bridge*
Upper Falls Bridge 73
Victorian Village Bridge 73
Village Bridge (Waitsfield) 75
Village Bridge (Waterville) – *see Church Street Bridge*
Waitsfield Bridge – *see Village Bridge (Waitsfield)*
Warren Bridge 75
West Arlington Bridge 77
West Dummerston Bridge 77
West Hill Bridge 78
Westford Bridge – *see Brown's River Bridge*
Whitecaps Bridge – *see Brookdale Bridge*
Wilder Bridge – *see Pine Brook Bridge*
Willard Bridge 78
Willard Twin Bridge 79
Williams River Bridge – *see Bartonsville Bridge*
Williamsville Bridge 79
Windsor-Cornish Bridge – *see Cornish-Windsor Bridge*
Witcomb Bridge – *see Chamberlin Mill Bridge*
Worrall Bridge 80
Vermont Covered Bridge Museum 81

RESOURCES 82

LIST OF ILLUSTRATIONS

KINGSLEY BRIDGE · East Clarendon ....frontispiece

FISHER RAILROAD BRIDGE · Wolcott / Hardwick 2

A.M. FOSTER BRIDGE · Cabot 10

COBURN BRIDGE · East Montpelier 20

EMILY'S BRIDGE · Stowe 26

GREEN RIVER BRIDGE · Guilford 30

JAYNES BRIDGE · Waterville 38

LONGLEY BRIDGE · Montgomery 44

CHURCH STREET BRIDGE · Waterville......................................50

POWER HOUSE BRIDGE · Johnson 56

HAMMOND BRIDGE · Pittsford 56

SHOREHAM RAILROAD BRIDGE · Shoreham..........................66

WARREN BRIDGE · Warren 74

WEST ARLINGTON BRIDGE · West Arlington..........................76

CORNISH-WINDSOR BRIDGE · Windsor....................................80

INTRODUCTION

Vermont once had more than 500 covered bridges. The goal of this book is to help you locate, visit and enjoy as many of the remaining ones as possible. Not only are the bridges themselves interesting and beautiful, but most are in scenic locations you might not find if not for them.

There have been many changes in recent decades. Several covered bridges were lost and a few new ones built. The most significant change is that many that were in disrepair and in danger of collapse—or of being bypassed—have been rehabilitated. The citizens of Vermont, along with their local and state governments, have invested mightily in these beloved and historic bridges.

An authentic covered bridge is one that was built from timber and features a truss or arch, which supports the roadway. The bridge is covered to protect the wood and enhance the structure's longevity.

This guide includes every existing authentic covered bridge in the state. In addition, there are some bridges that don't meet the foregoing definition, but are nonetheless of interest to many travelers. Those structures are often called "romantic shelters," and are designated as such here.

Many bridges are known by more than one name. The most "official" ones were selected; alternate names with referrals are also provided.

Construction dates cited for some bridges are approximate. Most standing bridges have been restored, often multiple times, and in a few cases were largely rebuilt. Many have had steel reinforcements added to accommodate modern vehicles, and some have been protected with metal roofs.

Included are bridges on private land, some of which are visible from the road. Seek landowner permission before entering private property. The status of bridges described as open to pedestrians or vehicles may change.

If you find conditions and information other than as described here, the author would greatly appreciate your comments. Please write or email:

Bella Terra Publishing
P.O. Box 731, Rhinebeck, NY 12572
marketing@bellaterramaps.com

FISHER RAILROAD BRIDGE • Wolcott / Hardwick

BRIDGE TRUSS FRAMES

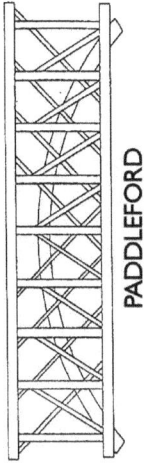

PADDLEFORD

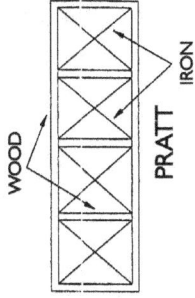

PRATT

WOOD

IRON

KINGPOST

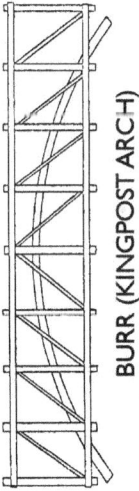

BURR (KINGPOST ARCH)

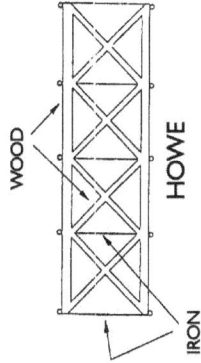

HOWE

WOOD

IRON

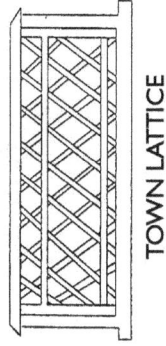

TOWN LATTICE

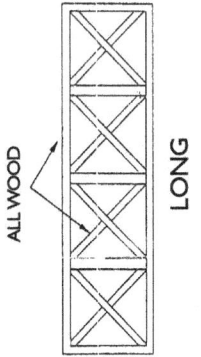

LONG

ALL WOOD

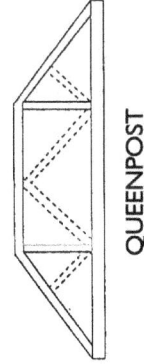

QUEENPOST

BRIDGE INDEX BY TOWN

To help you locate covered bridges near you, this listing shows bridge names by towns and localities they are in or adjacent to. Some bridges are listed more than once.

TOWN OR LOCALITY	BRIDGE NAME
Arlington	Chiselville
Arlington	West Arlington
Bakersfield	East Fairfield
Barre	Robbin's Nest
Bartonsville	Bartonsville
Bartonsville	Worrall
Bellows Falls	Hall
Bellows Falls	Victorian Village
Belvidere	Lumber Mill
Belvidere	Morgan
Bennington	Henry
Bennington	Paper Mill
Bennington	Silk
Brandon	Sanderson
Brattleboro	Creamery
Bridgewater	Lincoln
Brighton	Island Pond
Brownsville	Bowers
Cabot	A.M. Foster
Calais	Kent's Corner
Cambridge	Gates Farm
Cambridge	Grist Mill
Cambridge	Poland
Cambridgeport	Hitchcock-Cormier

TOWN OR LOCALITY	BRIDGE NAME
Charlotte	Holmes Creek
Charlotte	Quinlan
Charlotte	Seguin
Chelsea	Flint
Chelsea	Moxley
Clarendon	Brown
Clarendon	Kingsley
Columbia, NH	Columbia
Cornish, NH	Cornish-Windsor
Cornwall	Salisbury Station
Coventry	Orne
Danville	Greenbanks Hollow
Dover	Williamsville
Dummerston	West Dummerston
East Calais	Kent's Corner
East Clarendon	Kingsley
East Fairfield	East Fairfield
East Montpelier	Coburn
East Shoreham	Shoreham Railroad
Enosburg	Comstock
Enosburg	Hopkins
Fairfax	Maple Street
Fairfield	East Fairfield
Felchville	Ledoux Hometown
Ferrisburgh	Spade Farm
Florence	Hammond
Grafton	Cheddar
Grafton	Kidder Hill
Guilford	Green River

TOWN OR LOCALITY	BRIDGE NAME
Hardwick	Hisher Railroad
Hartford	Quechee
Hartland	Martin's Mill
Hartland	Willard
Hartland	Willard Twin
Irasburg	Lord's Creek
Irasburg	Orne
Irasburg	Village
Island Pond	Island Pond
Jeffersonville	Grist Mill
Jeffersonville	Poland
Johnson	Power House
Johnson	Scribner
Lancaster, NH	Mount Orne
Lemington	Columbia
Lunenberg	Mount Orne
Lyndon	Chamberlin Mill
Lyndon	Miller's Run
Lyndon	Randall
Lyndon	Sanborn
Lyndon	Schoolhouse
Lyndonville	Sanborn
Marlboro	Johnny Esau
Middlebury	Halpin
Middlebury	Pulp Mill
Mill Village	Best Western
Montgomery	Comstock
Montgomery	Fuller
Montgomery	Hopkins

TOWN OR LOCALITY	BRIDGE NAME
Montgomery	Hutchins
Montgomery	Longley
Montgomery	West Hill
Montpelier	Coburn
Morristown	Red
Moseley	Northfield
Newfane	Williamsville
North Clarendon	Brown
North Hartland	Willard
North Hartland	Willard Twin
Northfield	Chamberlin
Northfield Falls	Second
Northfield Falls	Slaughter House
Northfield Falls	Station
Northfield Falls	Third
Pittsford	Cooley
Pittsford	Depot
Pittsford	Gorham
Pittsford	Hammond
Plainfield	Coburn
Plainfield	Martin
Proctor	Cooley
Proctor	Gorham
Quechee	Quechee
Randolph	Braley
Randolph	Gifford
Randolph	Kingsbury
Reading	Ledoux Hometown
Rockingham	Bartonsville

TOWN OR LOCALITY	BRIDGE NAME
Rockingham	Hall
Rockingham	Hitchcock-Cormier
Rockingham	Victorian Village
Rockingham	Worrall
Roxbury	Chamberlin
Roxbury	Northfield
Royalton	Gifford
Royalton	Howe
Royalton	Kingsbury
Rutland	Twin
Salisbury	Salisbury Station
Shelburne	Shelburne Museum
Shoreham	Shoreham Railroad
Springfield	Baltimore
Stowe	Brookdale
Stowe	Emily's
Stowe	Red
Stowe	Stowe Walkway
Stratton Mountain	Snow
Sunderland	Chiselville
Taftsville	Taftsville
Thetford	Thetford Center
Thetford	Union Village
Townshend	Scott
Troy	River Road
Tunbridge	Cilley
Tunbridge	Flint
Tunbridge	Gifford
Tunbridge	Howe

TOWN OR LOCALITY	BRIDGE NAME
Tunbridge	Larkin
Tunbridge	Mill
Tunbridge	Moxley
Waitsfield	Battleground
Waitsfield	Pine Brook
Waitsfield	Village
Walden	A.M. Foster
Warren	Warren
Waterbury	Best Western
Waterville	Church Street
Waterville	Jayne's
Waterville	Montgomery
Weathersfield	Titcomb
Weathersfield	Salmond
Weathersfield	Upper Falls
West Arlington	West Arlington
West Brattleboro	Creamery
West Brattleboro	Green River
West Dummerston	West Dummerston
West Windsor	Best
West Windsor	Bowers
West Woodstock	Lincoln
Westford	Brown's River
White River Junction	Willard
White River Junction	Willard Twin
Whitingham	Corgi Crossing
Williamsville	Williamsville
Wilmington	Corgi Crossing
Wilmington	High Mowing Farm

TOWN OR LOCALITY	BRIDGE NAME
Windsor	Best
Windsor	Bowers
Windsor	Cornish-Windsor
Wolcott	Fisher Railroad
Woodstock	Frank Lewis
Woodstock	Lincoln
Woodstock	Middle
Woodstock	Taftsville
Woodstock	Teago

A.M. FOSTER BRIDGE • Cabot

THE BRIDGES

A.M. FOSTER BRIDGE
(1988)

Truss: Queenpost
Length: 40 ft
Crosses: manmade pond
Location: Cabot Plains Rd, off Rt 215, Cabot
GPS: 44.423475, -72.268286

Named for the builder's great-grandfather, inventor of the Foster Sap Spout. Replica of the Martin Bridge. Bridge is visible on right after the bend. Private.

BALTIMORE BRIDGE
(1870)

Truss: Town Lattice
Length: 44 ft
Crosses: drainage ditch
Location: Charlestown Rd/ Rt 11, off I-91 exit 7, Springfield
GPS: 43.270259, -72.448301

Relocated from the village of Baltimore in 1970. Adjacent to The Eureka Schoolhouse, 1790 one-room school. They comprise a State Historic Site. Open to pedestrians.

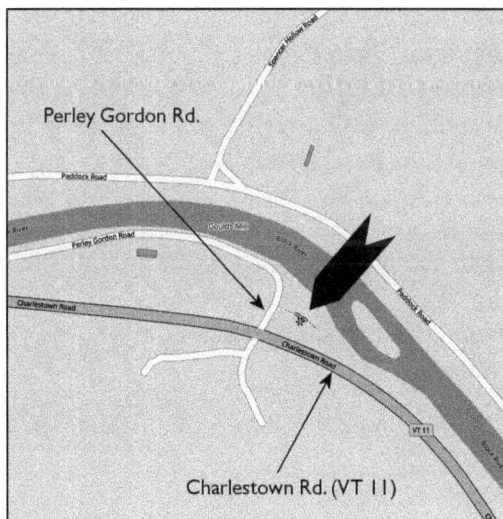

BARTONSVILLE BRIDGE (1870)

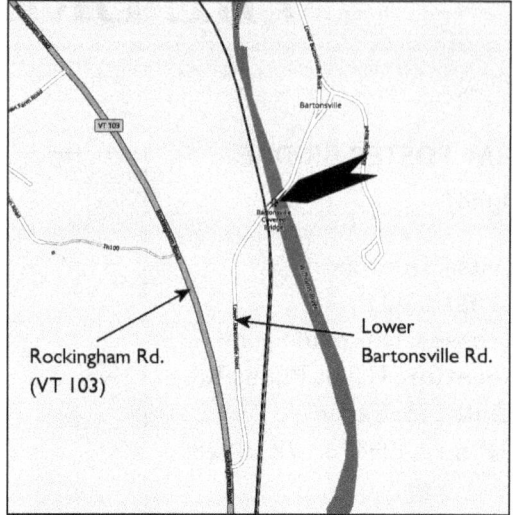

Rockingham Rd.
(VT 103)

Lower
Bartonsville Rd.

Truss: Town Lattice
Length: 151 ft
Crosses: Williams River
Location: Lower
Bartonsville Rd, off
Rockingham Rd/Rt 103,
Rockingham
GPS: 43.223977, -72.536749

Also known as Williams
River Bridge. One of
Vermont's longest covered
bridges. Hurricane Irene's
flood waters destroyed the bridge in 2011. It was rebuilt, and reopened in
2013. Listed on the National Register in 1973. Open to vehicles.

BATTLEGROUND BRIDGE (1974)

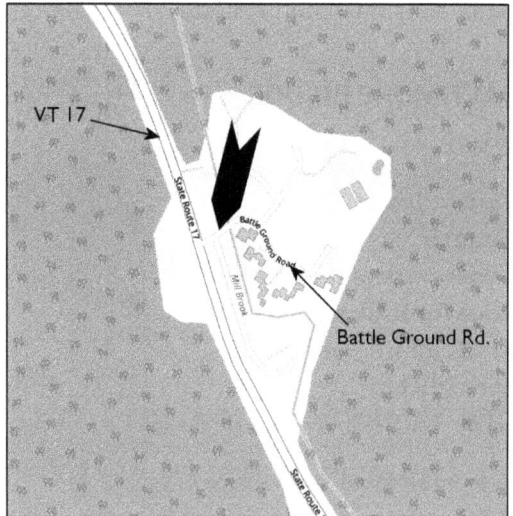

VT 17

Battle Ground Rd.

Romantic Shelter
Crosses: Mill Brook
Length: 51 ft
Location: Battleground
Resort, Rt 17/Mill Brook Rd,
Waitsfield
GPS: 44.200820, -72.894850

Open to vehicles; pedestrian
walkway.

BEST BRIDGE (1889)

Truss: Tied Arch
Length: 37 ft
Crosses: Mill Creek
Location: Churchill Rd, off
Rt 44, West Windsor
GPS: 43.455167, -72.516385

Named for a local family.
Also known as Swallows
Bridge for its builder. An
unusual tied arch truss of
laminated, bolted planks,
covered by a post and beam
shed. Listed on the National
Register in 1973. Open to vehicles.

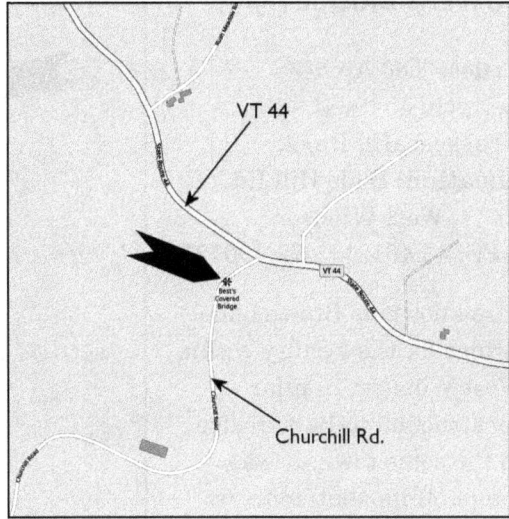

BEST WESTERN BRIDGE (1972)

Romantic Shelter
Crosses: unnamed brook
Length: 50 ft
Location: Blush Hill Rd, off
Rt 100/Waterbury Stowe
Rd, Waterbury
GPS: 44.345320, -72.749739

Open to pedestrians; behind
the Best Western Plus hotel.

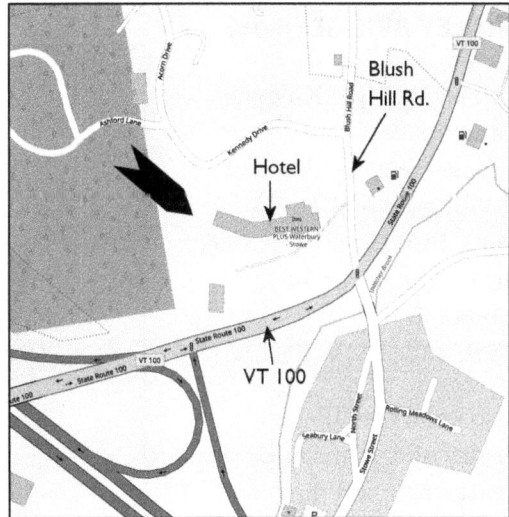

BOWERS BRIDGE (1919)

Truss: Tied Arch
Length: 45 ft
Crosses: Mill Brook
Location: Bible Hill Rd, off
Rt 44, West Windsor
GPS: 43.461347, -72.490727

Also known as Brownsville
Bridge for the locality within
West Windsor. Similar
construction to Best Bridge
in the same town. It was
swept off its abutments by
Hurricane Irene in 2011, but
rebuilt and reopened the following year. Listed on the National Register
in 1973. Open to vehicles.

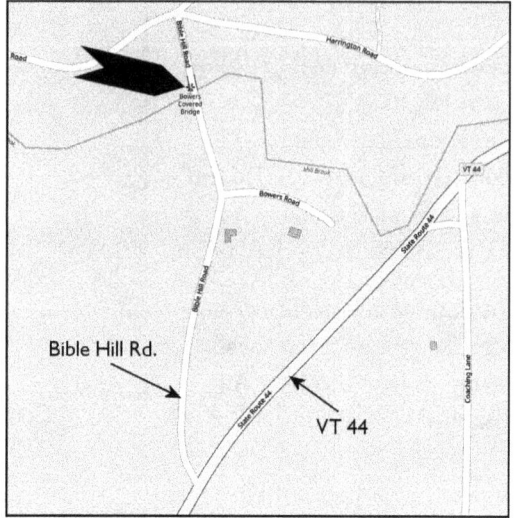

BRALEY BRIDGE (1904)

Truss: Multiple Kingpost
Length: 39 ft
Crosses: Second Branch
of White River
Location: Braley Covered
Bridge Rd, off Rt 14,
Randolph
GPS: 43.928519, -72.555172

Also known as Blaisdell
Bridge and Johnson Bridge.
Featuring a half-height
truss, the bridge was likely
built as an open deck "boxed
pony truss" bridge, and later covered, perhaps in 1909 per the date on the
portal. Listed on the National Register in 1974. Open to vehicles.

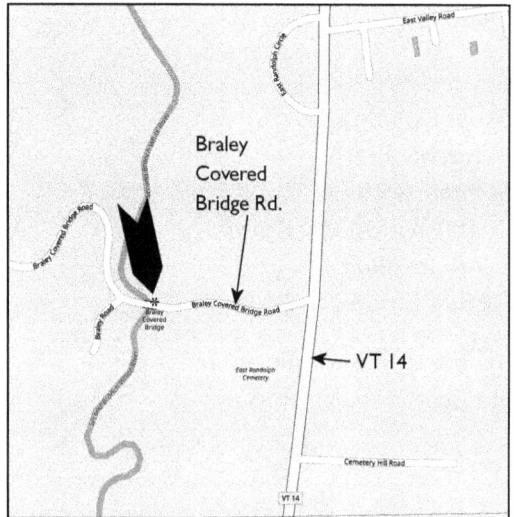

14

BROOKDALE BRIDGE (1970)

Romantic Shelter
Crosses: West Branch,
Waterbury River (aka West
Branch, Little River)
Length: 54 ft
Location: Brook Rd, off
Rt 108, Stowe
GPS: 44.497125, -72.745375

Also known as Whitecaps
Bridge. Open to vehicles.
Near parking for north end
of Stowe Recreation Path.

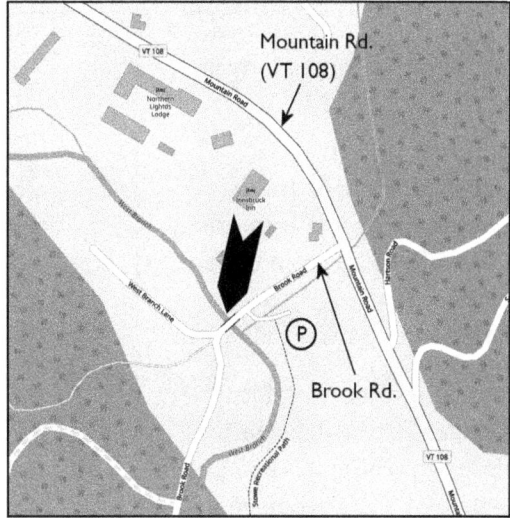

BROWN BRIDGE (1880)

Truss: Town Lattice
Length: 113 ft
Crosses: Cold River
Location: Upper Cold River
Rd, off Cold River Road, east
of North Clarendon
GPS: 43.566489, -72.918891

Also known as Hollow
Bridge. Very secluded. Listed
on the National Register in
1974. Designated National
Historic Landmark in 2014
as exemplar of Town Lattice

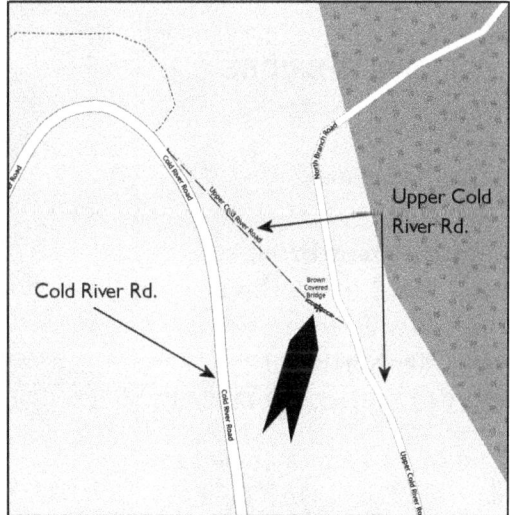

Truss construction. Possibly the only covered bridge which retains its
original slate roof. Open to vehicles. Road not maintained in winter.

BROWN'S RIVER BRIDGE (1838)

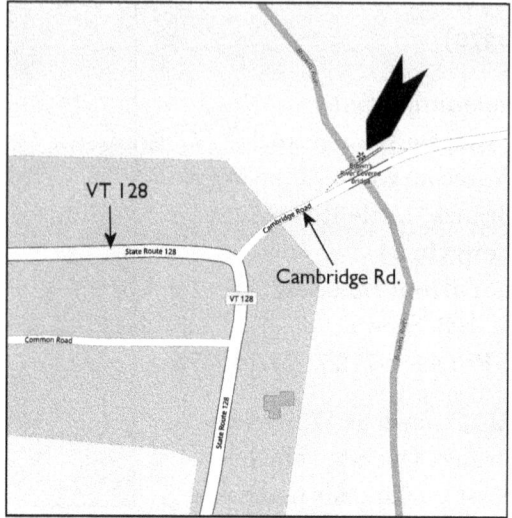

Truss: Burr Arch
Length: 97
Crosses: Browns River
Location: beside Cambridge Rd, Off Rt 128/Town Green, Westford
GPS: 44.612493, -73.008195

Also known as Westford Bridge. The bridge was closed to traffic in 1965 and bypassed. Later removed and repaired by Milton Graton, work documented in a National Geographic film. It was returned to its original location and rededicated in 2001. Open to pedestrians.

CHAMBERLIN BRIDGE (1956)

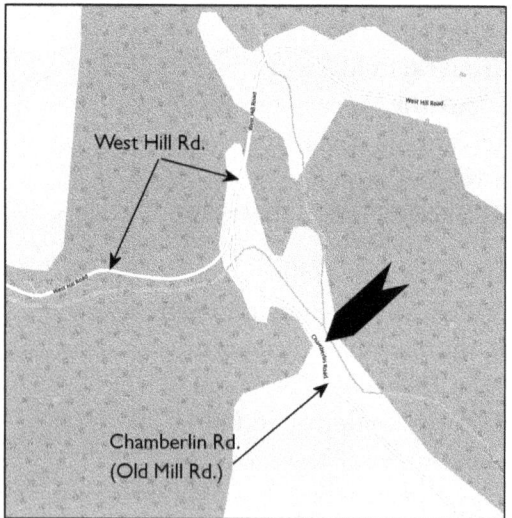

Truss: Kingpost
Length: 22 ft
Crosses: Stony Brook
Location: Chamberlin Rd (aka Old Mill Rd), off Stony Brook Rd, Northfield
GPS: 44.148766, -72.718246

Built by Mahlon Chamberlin to provide access to a field behind his house. Visible from road. Private.

CHAMBERLIN MILL BRIDGE (1881)

Truss: Queenpost
Length: 69 ft
Crosses: South Wheelock
Branch of Passumpsic River
Location: Chamberlin
Bridge Rd, between S
Wheelock Rd and York St,
Lyndon
GPS: 44.516416, -72.016594

Also known as Chamberlin
Bridge and Witcomb Bridge.
Possibly built as an
uncovered bridge and covered in 1881. Listed on the National Register in
1974. Open to vehicles.

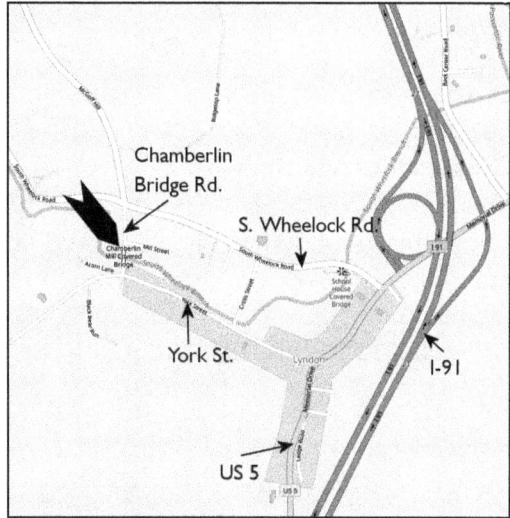

CHEDDAR BRIDGE (1967)

Romantic Shelter
Crosses: South Branch,
Saxton River
Length: 62 ft
Location: Grafton Village
Cheese Company, Grafton
Rd (aka Townshend Rd),
Grafton
GPS: 43.166273, -72.613069

Also known as MacMillan
Bridge. Open to pedestrians.

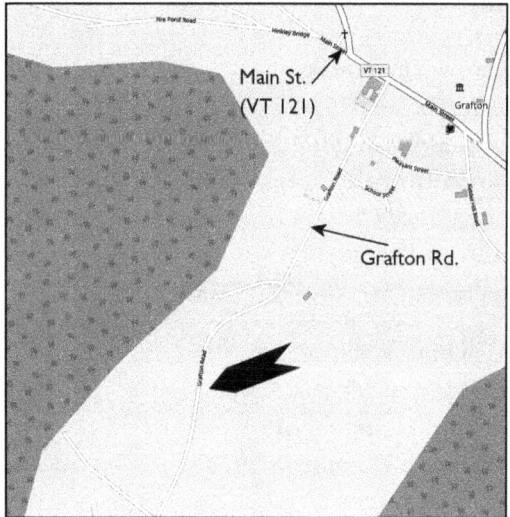

CHISELVILLE BRIDGE
(1870)

Truss: Town Lattice
Length: 117 feet
Crosses: Roaring Branch
Brook
Location: Sunderland Hill
Rd, south of Rt 7A,
Sunderland
GPS: 43.072122, -73.133313

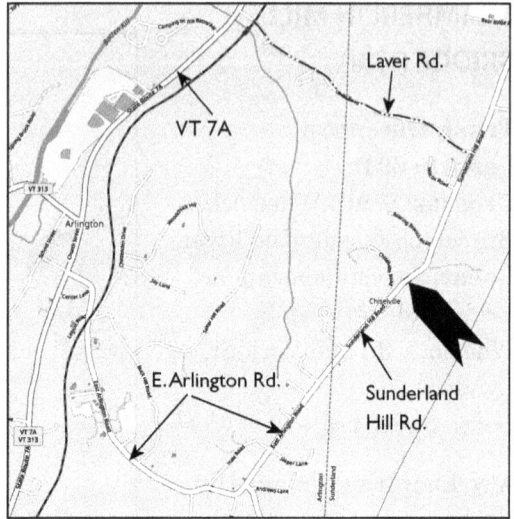

Named for a former chisel
factory. Also known as
Roaring Branch Bridge. Sits 40 feet above brook. Sign at entrance: "One
dollar fine for driving faster than a walk on this bridge." Open to vehicles.

CHURCH STREET BRIDGE
(1877)

Truss: Queenpost
Length: 61 ft
Crosses: Lamoille River,
North Branch
Location: Church St, off Rt
109, Waterville
GPS: 44.690123, -72.771006

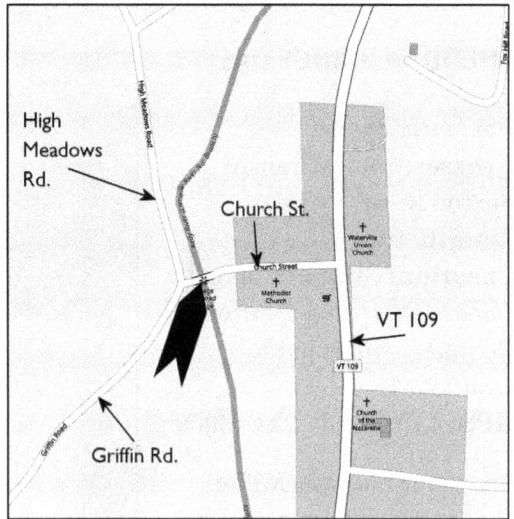

Also known as Village
Bridge and Meat Market
Bridge. Listed on the
National Register in 1974.
Open to vehicles.

18

CILLEY BRIDGE (1883)

Truss: Multiple Kingpost
Length: 66 ft
Crosses: First Branch
of White River
Location: Howe Lane, off Rt
110, Tunbridge
GPS: 43.882977, -72.503899

As with two other bridges
crossing this branch, the
portals are skewed, creating
a slight camber. Listed on
the National Register in
1974. Open to vehicles.

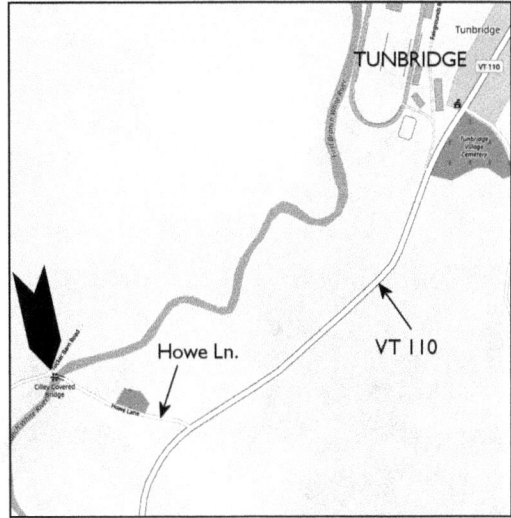

COBURN BRIDGE (1851)

Truss: Queenpost
Length: 69 ft
Crosses: Winooski River
Location: Coburn Rd, off Rt
2 or Rt 14, East Montpelier
GPS: 44.280817, -72.454207

Also known as Cemetery
Bridge. Built by Larned
Coburn at no cost to the
town in exchange for having
the road pass by his house.
Listed on the National
Register in 1974. Open to
vehicles.

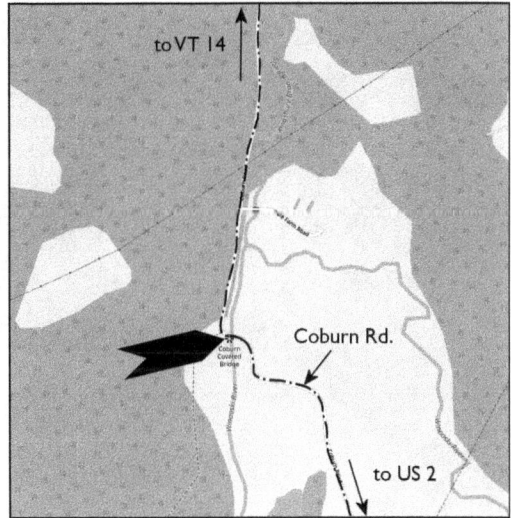

COBURN BRIDGE • East Montpelier

COLUMBIA BRIDGE (1912)

Truss: Howe
Length: 146 ft
Crosses: Connecticut River
Location: Columbia Bridge
Rd, off Rt 102/River Rd,
Lemington.
GPS: 44.853125, -71.551602

Connects Lemington to
Columbia, NH. Built at the
end of Vermont's historic
covered bridge era. Replaced
a bridge that stood for just
one year before being
destroyed by fire. Downstream side is fully covered, while the upstream
side is half covered and lets in light. Listed on the National Register in
1976. Open to vehicles.

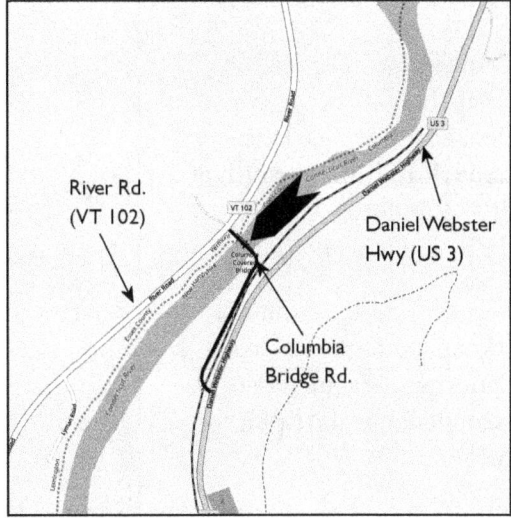

COMSTOCK BRIDGE (1883)

Truss: Town Lattice
Length: 69 ft
Crosses: Trout River
Location: Comstock Bridge
Rd, off Rt 118, Montgomery
GPS: 44.899694, -72.644600

Named for a local
millwright. Listed on the
National Register in
1974.Open to vehicles.

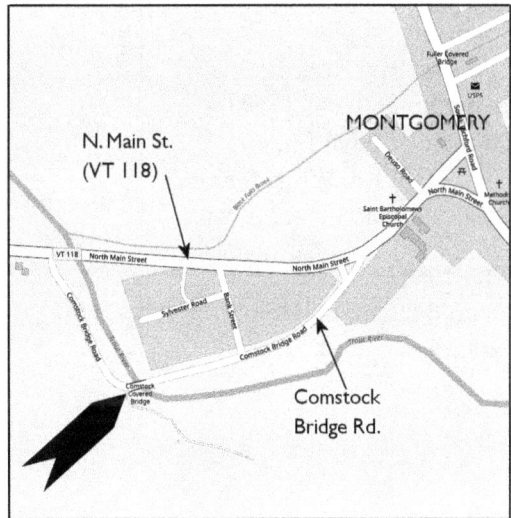

COOLEY BRIDGE (1849)

Truss: Town Lattice
Length: 60 ft
Crosses: Furnace Brook
Location: Elm St, south of
Rt 7, Pittsford
GPS: 43.690417, -73.028563

Named for a local family.
Often said to resemble a
Conestoga Wagon due to its
extended portals. Open to
vehicles.

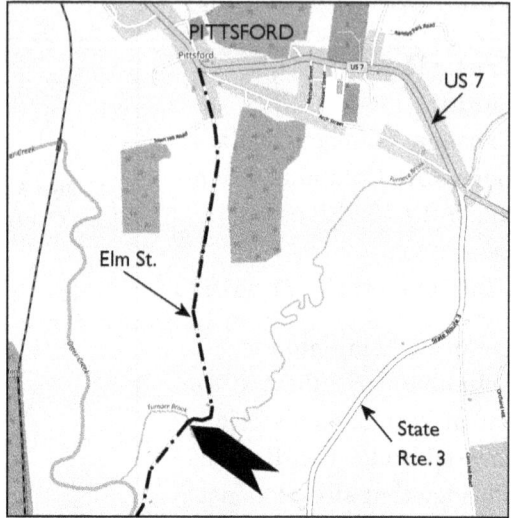

CORGI CROSSING BRIDGE (2006)

Romantic Shelter
Crosses: Big Rock Brook
Length: 26 ft
Location: Boyd Ln, off
Fuller Hill Rd, Whitingham
GPS: 42.825033, -72.862400

This 1984 bridge was
covered 22 years later.
Private.

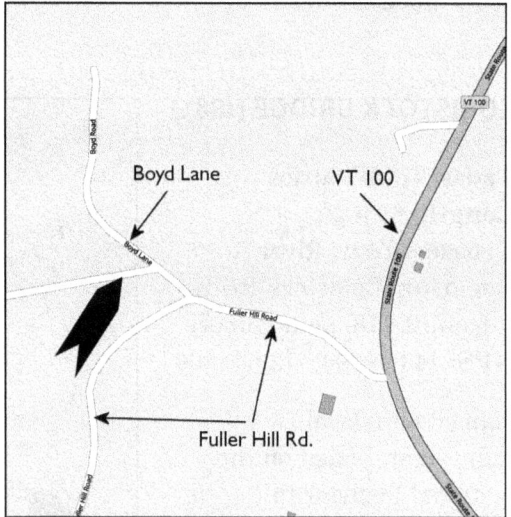

CORNISH-WINDSOR BRIDGE (1866)

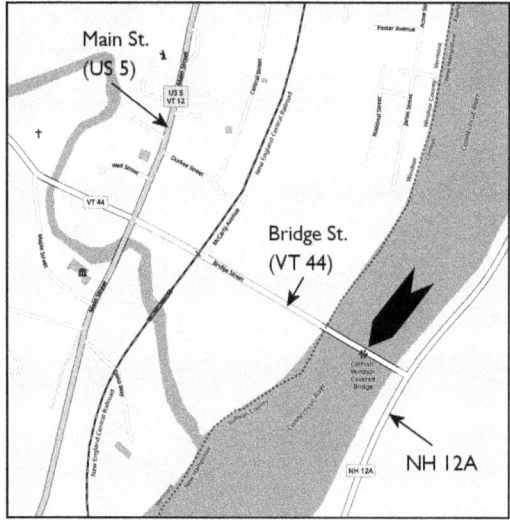

Truss: Town Lattice
Length: 449 ft
Crosses: Connecticut River
Location: Bridge St/Rt 44,
off Rt 5, Windsor
GPS: 43.473609, -
72.384024

Also known as Windsor-
Cornish Bridge. Connects
Windsor to Cornish, NH.
Beyond the Vermont shore,
the bridge is in New Hampshire, with parking on that side. The longest
historic covered bridge in the U.S. Designated a National Civil
Engineering Landmark in 1970. Listed on the National Register in 1976.
Open to vehicles.

CREAMERY BRIDGE (BRATTLEBORO) (1879)

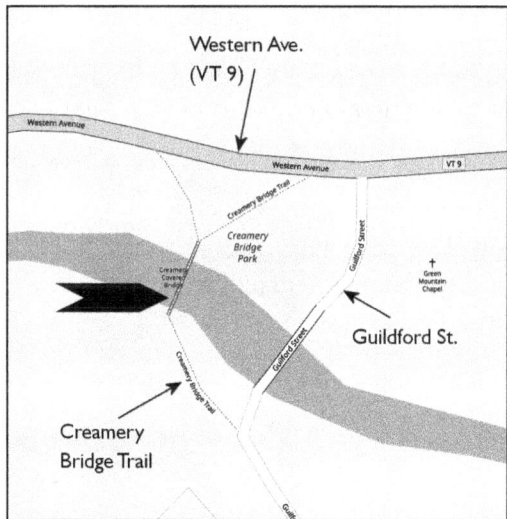

Truss: Town Lattice
Length: 80 ft
Crosses: Whetstone Brook
Location: Guilford St, off
Rt 9, Brattleboro.
GPS: 42.849739,-72.585809

Walkway added in 1917.
Listed on the National
Register in 1973. Guilford St
bypasses the bridge which is
open to pedestrians.
Adjacent to Living Memorial Park.

DEPOT BRIDGE (1840)

Truss: Town Lattice
Length: 121 ft
Crosses: Otter Creek
Location: Depot Hill Rd, off
Rt 7, Pittsford
GPS: 43.709523, -73.042715

Also known as Florence
Station Bridge. Listed on the
National Register in
1974.Open to vehicles.

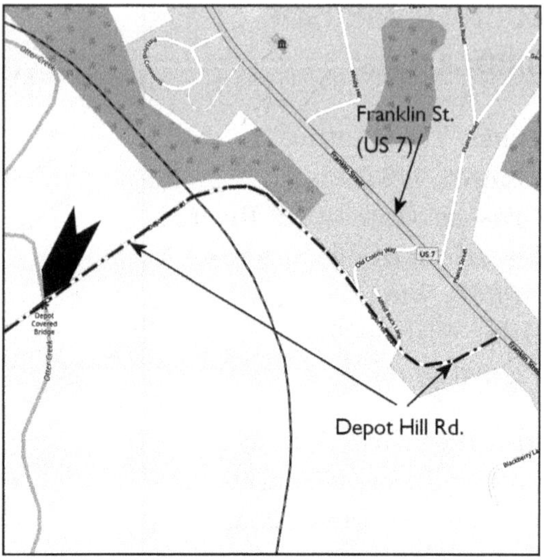

EAST FAIRFIELD BRIDGE (1865)

Truss: Queenpost
Length: 67 ft
Crosses: Black Creek
Location: Bridge St, off Rt
36, East Fairfield
GPS: 44.786095, -72.862373

Once surrounded by mills
and other industries. Listed
on the National Register in
1974. Open to vehicles.

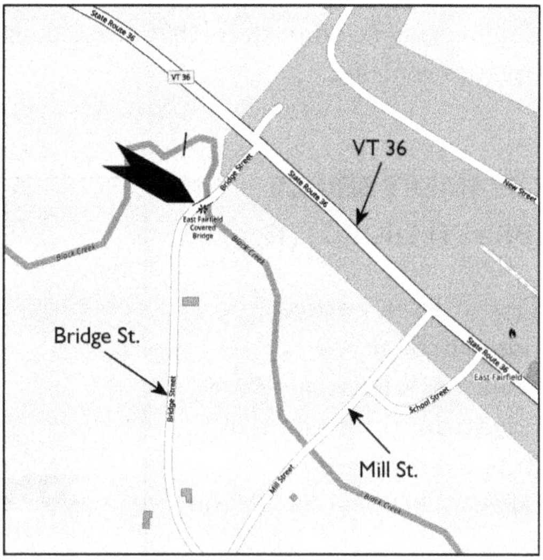

EMILY'S BRIDGE (1844)

Truss: Howe
Length: 48 ft
Crosses: Gold Brook
Location: Covered Bridge
Rd, off Gold Brook Rd, east
of Waterbury Rd/Rt 100,
Stowe
GPS: 44.440429, -72.679872

Also known as Gold Brook
Bridge and Stone Hollow
Bridge. It is the state's only
surviving example of a Howe
truss in timber on a public roadway. Named for a ghost that is reputed to
shake cars and claw pedestrians. Listed on the National Register in
1974.Open to vehicles, if you dare.

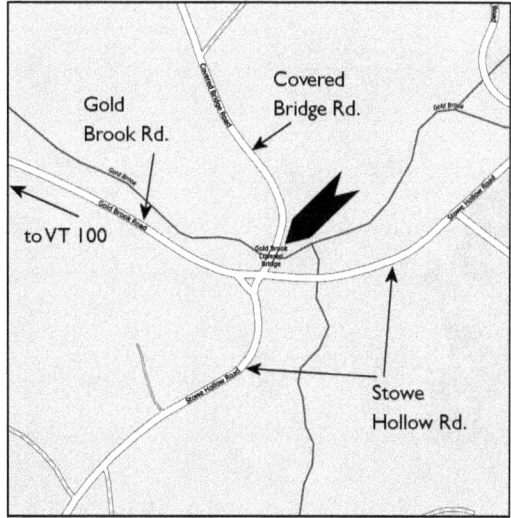

FISHER RAILROAD BRIDGE (1908)

Truss: Double Town Lattice
Length: 103 ft
Crosses: Lamoille River
Location: Rt 15, between
Wolcott and Hardwick
GPS: 44.532290, -72.427702

Also known as Chubb
Bridge. Built for the St.
Johnsbury & Lamoille
County Railroad, it was the
last covered bridge in
Vermont to carry rail traffic. Unique full-length cupola vented smoke
from steam locomotives. Listed on the National Register in 1974.
Roadside park and observation deck on south side of road.

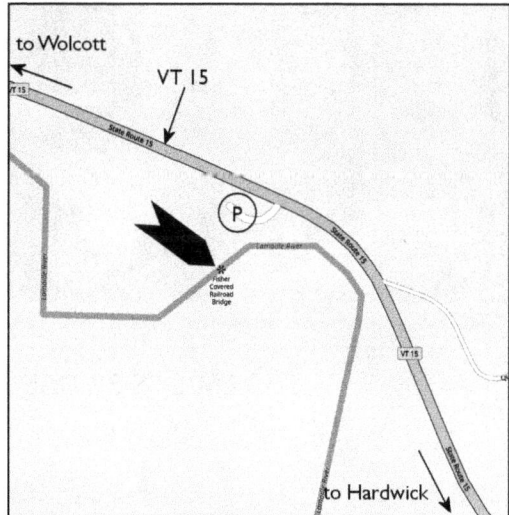

EMILY'S BRIDGE • Stowe

FLINT BRIDGE (1845)

Truss: Queenpost
Length: 87 ft
Crosses: First Branch
of White River
Location: Bicknell Hill Rd,
off Rt 110, Tunbridge
GPS: 43.949335, -72.458680

The oldest of 6 covered
bridges crossing the First
Branch in a 7 mile stretch.
Listed on the National
Register in 1974. Open to
vehicles.

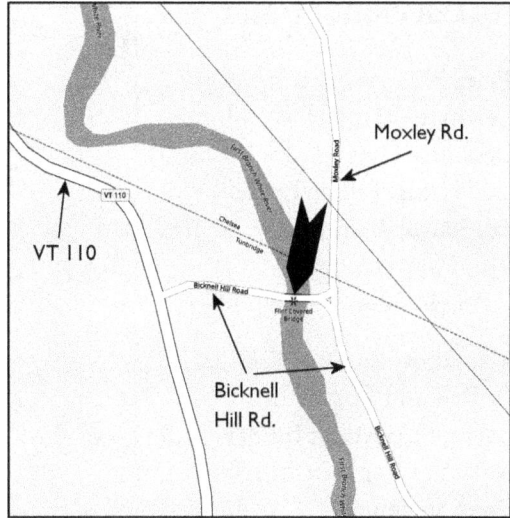

FRANK LEWIS BRIDGE (1981)

Truss: Custom Kingpost &
Town Lattice Variation
Length: 40 ft
Crosses: Gulf Stream
Location: Barnard Rd/Rt
12, north of Rt 4, Woodstock
GPS: 43.653545, -72.565400

Named for the farmer who
built it at age 61, the bridge
is truly homemade in design
and construction. Visible on
west side of road. Private.

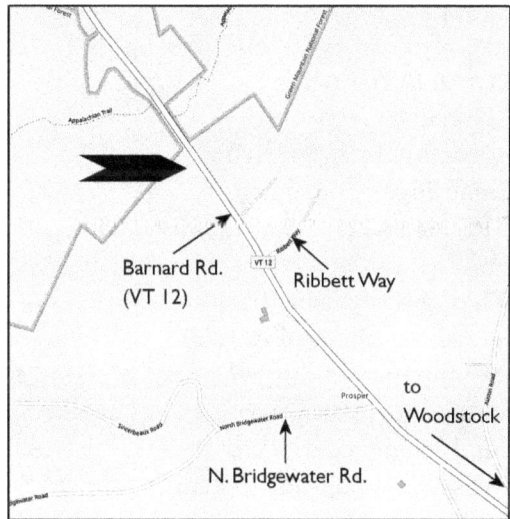

FULLER BRIDGE (1890)

Truss: Town Lattice
Length: 50 ft
Crosses: Black Falls Brook
Location: Fuller Bridge
Rd/South Richford Rd, off Rt
118, Montgomery
GPS: 44.903281, -72.639737

Also known as Black Falls
Bridge and Post Office
Bridge. Listed on the
National Register in 1974.
Open to vehicles.

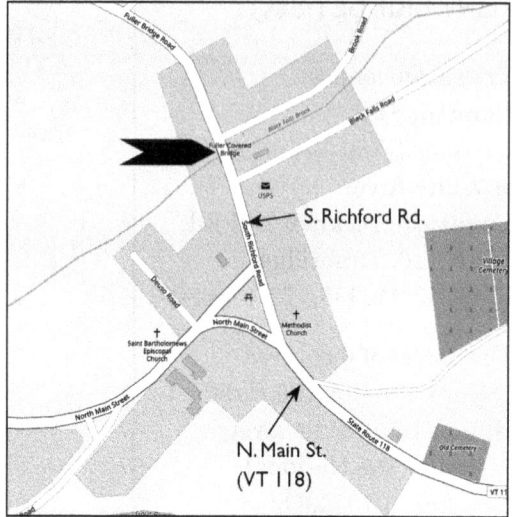

GATES FARM BRIDGE (1897)

Truss: Burr Arch
Length: 83 ft
Location: farm, off Rt 15,
Cambridge
GPS: 44.645744, -72.872336

When the Seymour River's
course was changed in 1950,
the state moved this bridge
to the Gates Farm so the
family could again have
access to its fields. Listed on

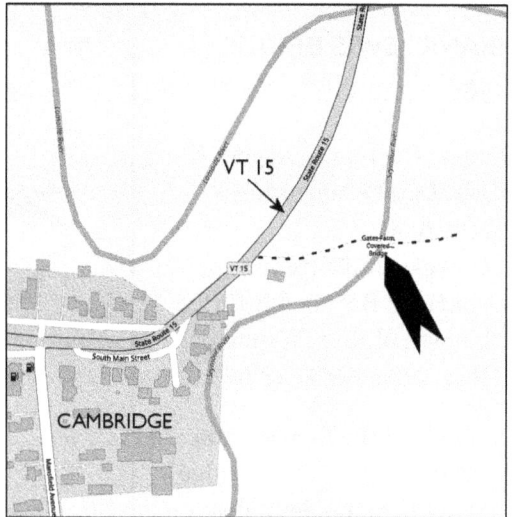

the National Register in 1974. Visible from Rt 15 north of Cambridge
village. Private.

GIFFORD BRIDGE (1904)

Truss: Multiple Kingpost
Length: 52 ft
Crosses: Second Branch
of White River
Location: Hyde Rd, off Rt
14, Randolph
GPS: 43.916179, -72.554990

Also known as C.K. Smith
Bridge. Like the nearby
Braley Bridge, it was
originally built as an
uncovered half-height
multiple kingpost truss "boxed pony bridge." Above that was later built a
kingpost within queenpost and roof. Listed on the National Register in
1974. Open to vehicles.

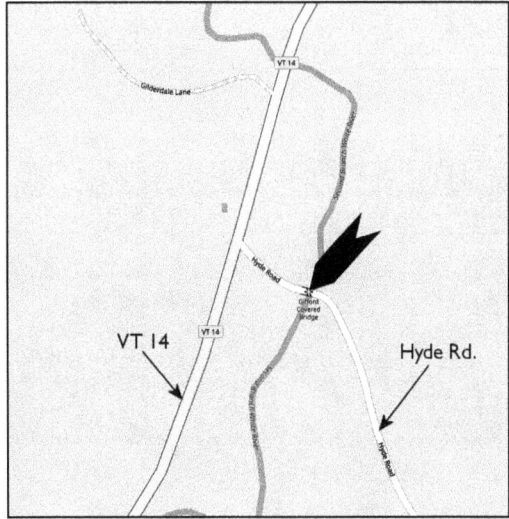

GORHAM BRIDGE (1841)

Truss: Town Lattice
Length: 114 ft
Crosses: Otter Creek
Location: Gorham Bridge
Rd, off Rt3 or Elm St, Proctor
GPS: 43.680064, -73.037460

Also known as Goodnough
Bridge. Washed downstream
in 1927 flood, but survived
and was returned to service.
Listed on the National
Register in 1974. Open to
vehicles

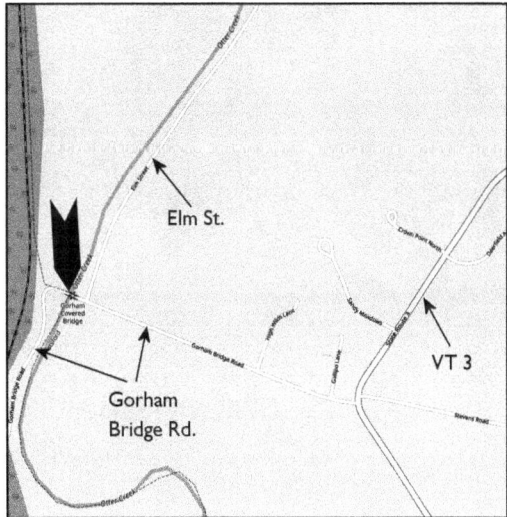

GREEN RIVER BRIDGE • Guilford

GREEN RIVER BRIDGE (1870)

Truss: Town Lattice
Length: 105 ft
Crosses: Green River
Location: (Jacksonville)
Stage Rd, between
intersections with River Rd
and Green River Rd, Guilford
GPS: 42.775459, -72.667173

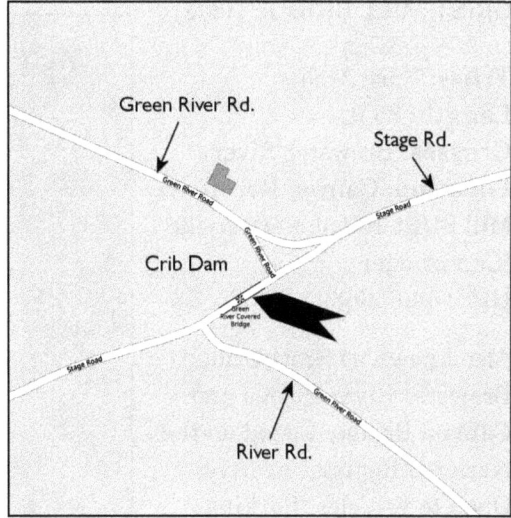

Local residents' mailboxes
were once sheltered inside
the bridge. Listed on the
National Register in 1973. Open to vehicles. Just upriver is the historic
Green River Crib Dam.

GREENBANKS HOLLOW BRIDGE (1886)

Truss: Queenpost
Length: 74 ft
Crosses: Joe's Brook
Location: Brainerd St, off
Rt 2, to Greenbanks Hollow
Rd, Danville
GPS: 44.377583, -72.121991

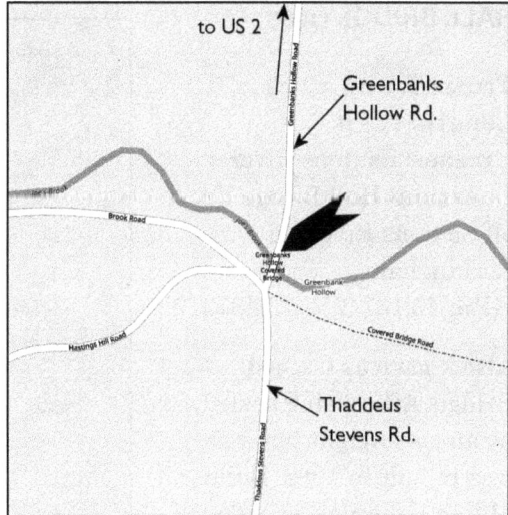

Built after a fire destroyed
Benjamin Greenbank's
"company town", including a
woolen mill, store and a
bridge. Ruins of the mill and some buildings can be seen. Listed on the
National Register in 1974. Significantly rebuilt in 2002.Open to vehicles.

GRIST MILL BRIDGE (1872)

Truss: Burr Arch
Length: 85 ft
Crosses: Brewster River
Location: Canyon Rd, off
Mill St/Rt 108, Jeffersonville
(Cambridge)
GPS: 44.636682, -72.825326

Also known as Scott Bridge,
Brewster River Bridge and
Canyon Bridge. Listed on the
National Register in 1974.
Open to vehicles. Parking
area for Brewster River
Gorge trail.

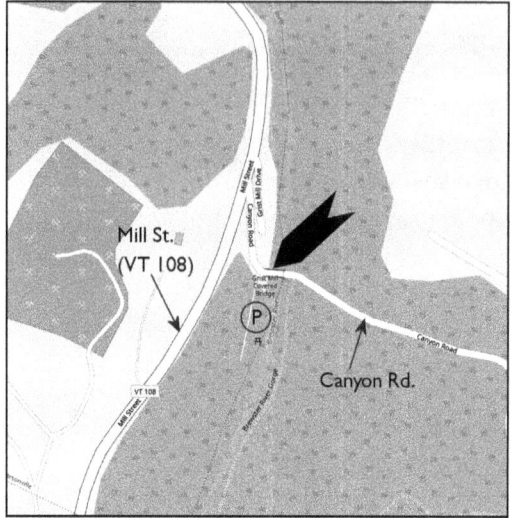

HALL BRIDGE (1867)

Truss: Town Lattice
Length: 121 ft
Crosses: Saxtons River
Location: Hall Bridge Rd,
off Saxtons River Rd,
Rockingham
GPS: 43.137425, -72.487319

Also known as Osgood
Bridge. After being destroyed
by an overweight truck, it
was rebuilt in 1982. Builder
Milton Graton used oxen to
move the bridge into place as
was done in the 19th century. Listed on the National Register in 1973.
Open to vehicles.

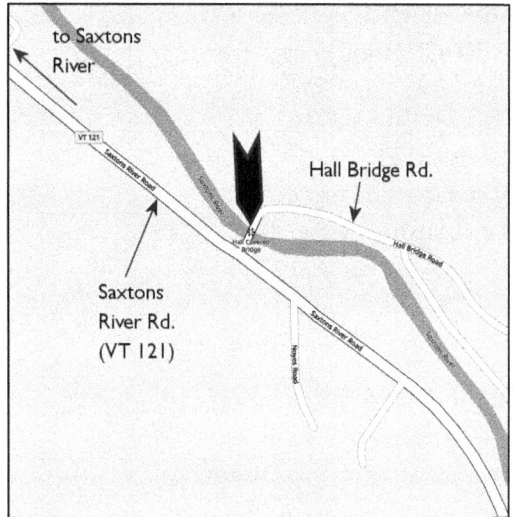

HALPIN BRIDGE (1850)

Truss: Town Lattice
Length: 66 feet
Crosses: Muddy Branch of
New Haven River
Location: Halpin Covered
Bridge Rd, off Halpin Rd,
east of Rt 7, Middlebury
GPS: 44.0500120, -73.140702

Also known as High Bridge.
Built to serve a marble
quarry, it is the covered
bridge highest above
waterway in Vermont, 41 ft
above Muddy Branch. Unverified claims date it to 1824.Listed on the
National Register in 1974. Bridge serves a private farm. Open to vehicles.

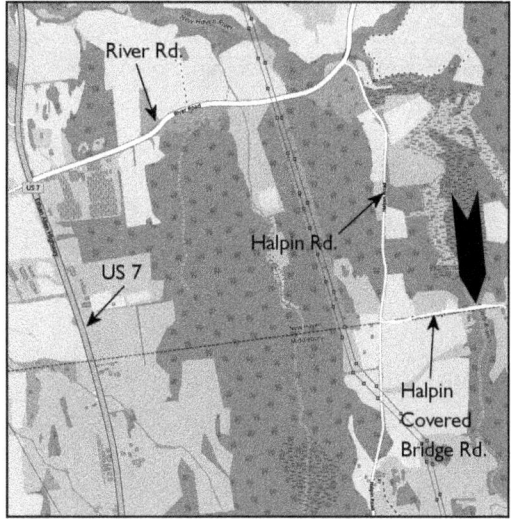

HAMMOND BRIDGE (1842)

Truss: Town Lattice
Length: 139 ft
Crosses: Otter Creek
Location: Kendall Hill Rd,
off Rt 7, Pittsford
GPS: 43.720682, -73.053477

Washed downstream in 1927
flood, but survived and was
returned to service. Listed on
National Register in 1974.
Road now bypasses the
bridge. Good picnic spot.
Open to pedestrians.

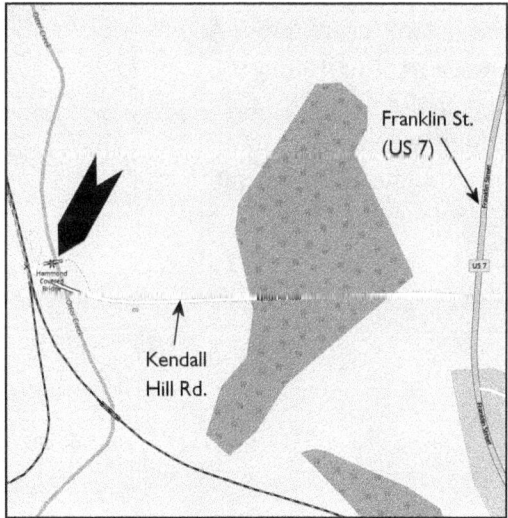

HECTORVILLE BRIDGE (1883)

Truss: Town Lattice & Kingpost
Length: 53 ft

Also known as Gibou Road Bridge for its second and most recent location. Dismantled and in storage at press time. A local Montgomery group hopes to have it restored and relocated. Listed on the National Register in 1974.

HENRY BRIDGE (1989)

Truss: Town Lattice
Length: 121 ft.
Crosses: Walloomsac River
Location: Murphy Rd, south of Harrington Rd/River Rd, Bennington
GPS: 42.912508, -73.254588

Named for local family. Also known as Burt Henry Bridge. Replica of 1840 bridge, which was listed on the National Register in 1973. Open to vehicles.

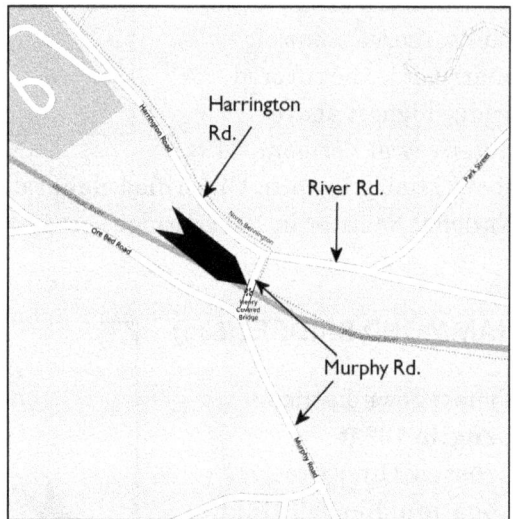

HIGH MOWING FARM BRIDGE (1949)

Truss: Town Lattice
Length: 22 ft
Crosses: Stowe Brook
Location: Stowe Hill Rd, off Rt 100, Wilmington
GPS: 42.882752, -72.850418

Bridge was built so a farm's herd of sheep could access fields for grazing. Bridge visible in valley on right, about a mile up Stowe Hill Road. Private.

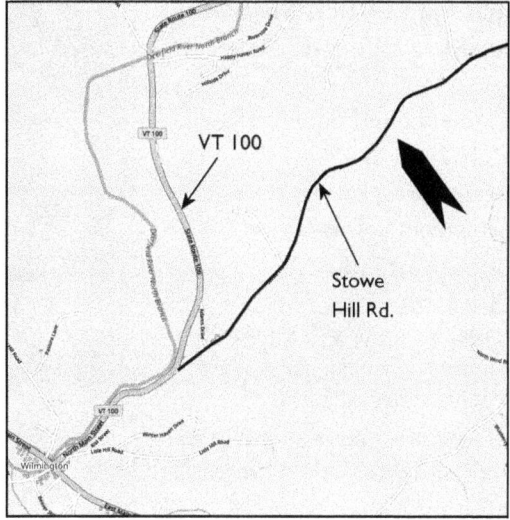

HITCHCOCK-CORMIER BRIDGE (2008)

Truss: Town Lattice
Length: 22 ft
Crosses: Weaver Brook
Location: 105 Atcherson Hollow Rd, Cambridgeport
GPS: 43.161488, -72.55163

Designed by Gerry Cormier and built by Raymond Hitchcock on his property. Parking at base of front lawn at beginning of rock wall. Private; request permission to visit.

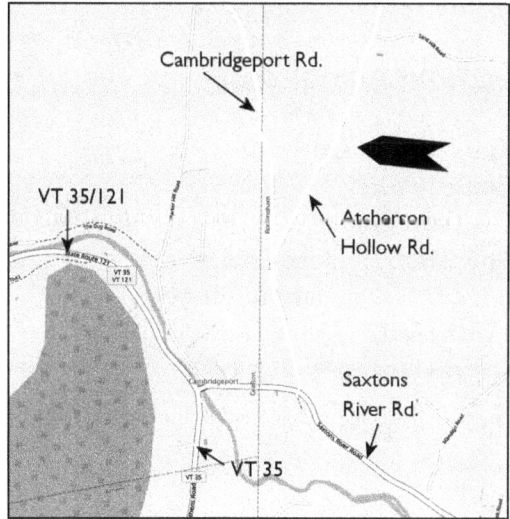

35

HOLMES CREEK BRIDGE (1870)

Truss: King Post with tied arch
Length: 41 ft
Crosses: Holmes Creek
Location: Lake Rd, Charlotte
GPS: 44.333123, -73.282301

At the shore of Lake Champlain. Named for local apple growers who operated what may have been the largest orchard in New England. Boats docked nearby to transport the fruit. Also known as Lake Shore Bridge and Holmes Bridge. Swimming area nearby. Listed on the National Register in 1974. Open to vehicles.

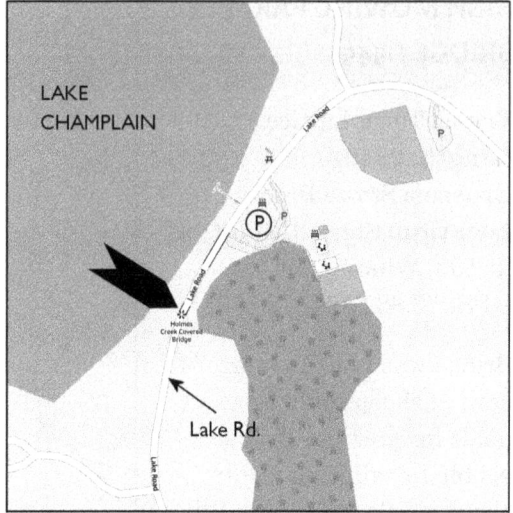

HOPKINS BRIDGE (1875)

Truss: Town Lattice
Length: 91 ft
Crosses: Trout River
Location: Hopkins Bridge Rd, off Montgomery Rd/Rt 118, Enosburg
GPS: 44.920615, -72.672980

Closed in 1993, it was rehabilitated and reopened in 1999 at a cost of more than $300,000 although it serves a single farm. Listed on the National Register in 1974.Open to vehicles.

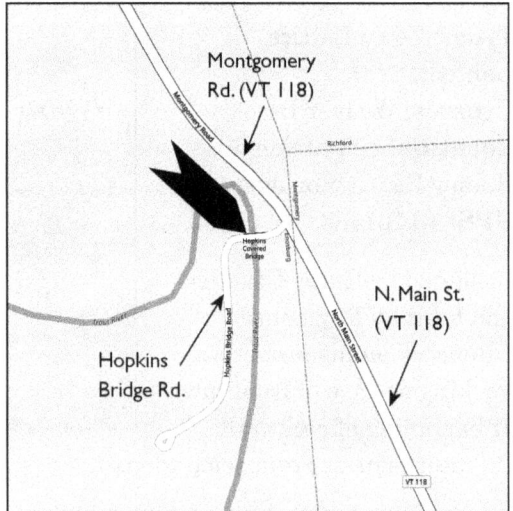

HOWE BRIDGE (1879)

Truss: Multiple Kingpost
Length: 75 ft
Crosses: First Branch
of White River
Location: Belknap Brook
Rd, off Rt 110, Tunbridge
GPS: 43.864897, -72.499054

Named for a local family,
many of whom are still in
the vicinity. Listed on the
National Register in 1974.
Open to vehicles.

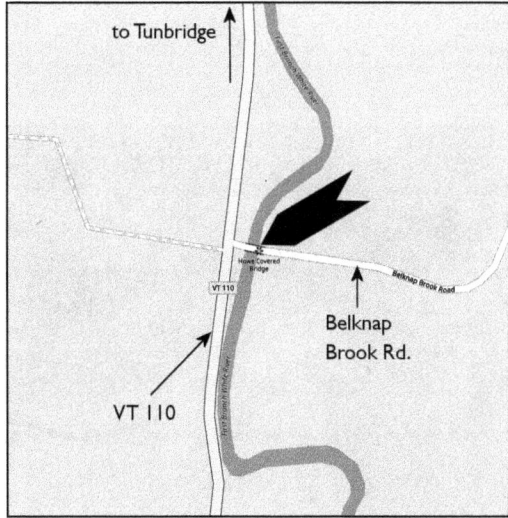

HUTCHINS BRIDGE (1883)

Truss: Town Lattice
Length: 77 ft
Crosses: Trout River, South
Branch
Location: Hutchins Bridge
Rd, off South Main St/Rt
118, Montgomery
GPS: 44.858596, -72.612536

Stands next to ruins of
Joseph Hutchins' butter tub
factory. Listed on the
National Register in 1974.
Open to vehicles.

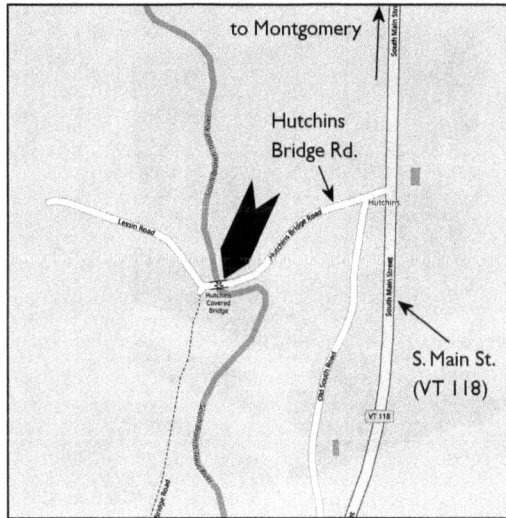

JAYNES BRIDGE • Waterville

ISLAND POND FOOTBRIDGE (2003)

Truss: Howe
Length: 242 ft
Crosses: railroad tracks
Location: Jct of Rts 105 &
114, Island Pond
GPS: 44.816295, -71.88105

A unique covered pedestrian
bridge crossing railroad
tracks by the historic former
Grand Trunk Railway depot.

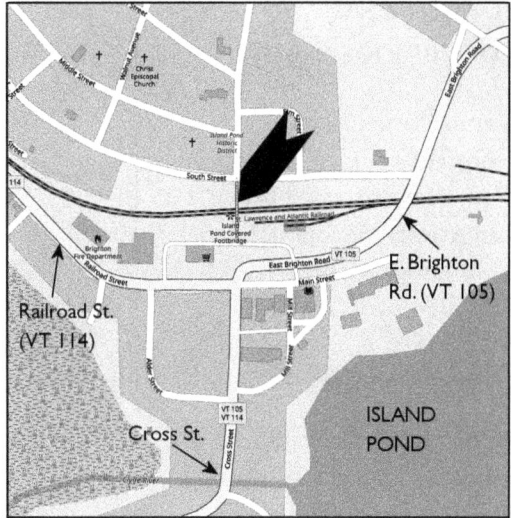

JAYNES BRIDGE (1877)

Truss: Queenpost
Length: 57 ft
Crosses: Lamoine River,
North Branch
Location: Codding Hollow
Rd, off Rt 109, Waterville
GPS: 44.712094, -72.756211

Named for a local family.
Also known as Codding
Hollow Bridge and Kissing
Bridge. Listed on the
National Register in 1974.
Open to vehicles.

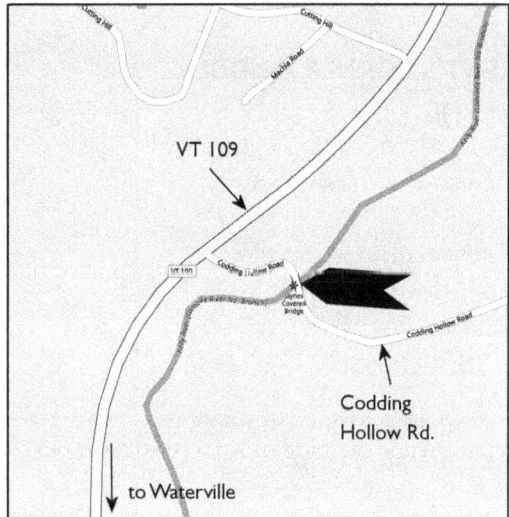

39

JOHNNY ESAU FOOTBRIDGE (2004)

Truss: Town Lattice
Length: 15 ft
Crosses: unnamed brook
Location: Marlboro
Elementary School, Rt
9/Molly Stark Trail,
Marlboro
GPS: 42.869226, -72.719675

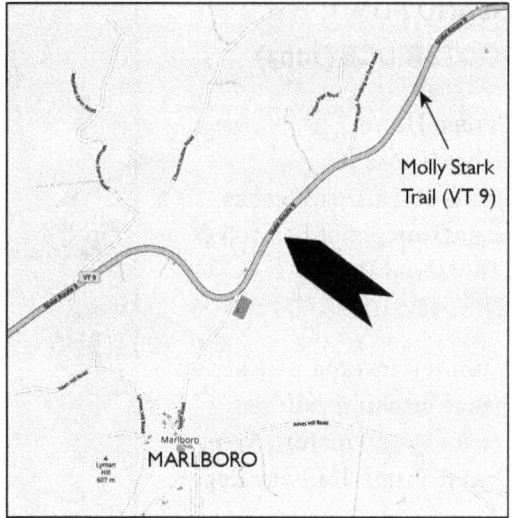

Built by fourth grade
students as a class project
under direction of their
teacher, Mr. Esau, who passed away in 2018.

KENT'S CORNER BRIDGE (1994)

Truss: Kingpost
Length: 23 ft
Crosses: Curtis Brook
Location: Kent Hill Rd,
East Calais
GPS: 44.368350, - 72.483433

Visible in meadow on north
side of road. Private.

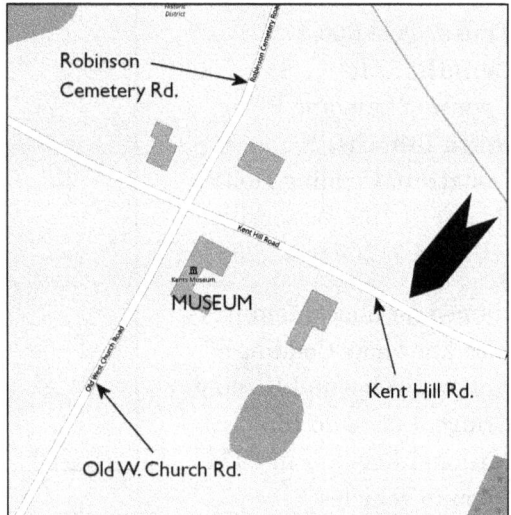

KIDDER HILL BRIDGE (1870)

Truss: Kingpost
Length: 66 ft
Crosses: Saxtons River,
South Branch
Location: Kidder Hill Rd,
off Main St/Rt 121, Grafton
GPS: 43.169130, -72.605359

Vermont's longest Kingpost
bridge. Listed on the
National Register in 1973.
Open to vehicles.

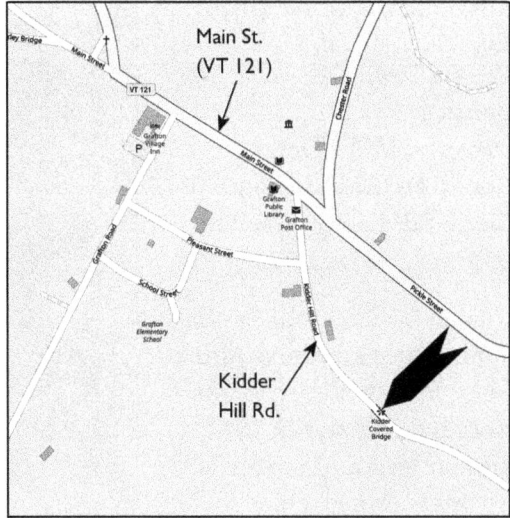

KINGSBURY BRIDGE (1904)

Truss: Multiple Kingpost
Length: 51 ft
Crosses: Second Branch
of White River
Location: Kingsbury Rd, off
Rt 14, Randolph
GPS: 43.880817, -72.581963

Also known as Hyde Bridge
and South Randolph Bridge.
Features curved portals. X-
bracing to the roof and curbs
at the floor were added in
2009. Listed on the National
Register in 1974. Open to vehicles.

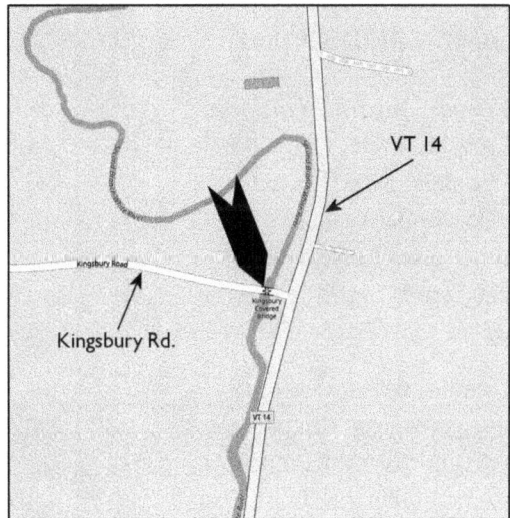

KINGSLEY BRIDGE (1836)

Truss: Town Lattice
Length: 121 ft
Crosses: Mill River
Location: East St, south of
Gorge Rd, East Clarendon
GPS: 43.523794, -72.940915

Named for local mill owning
family. Also known as Mill
River Bridge. Listed on the
National Register in 1974.
Former gristmill nearby is
privately owned. Open to
vehicles.

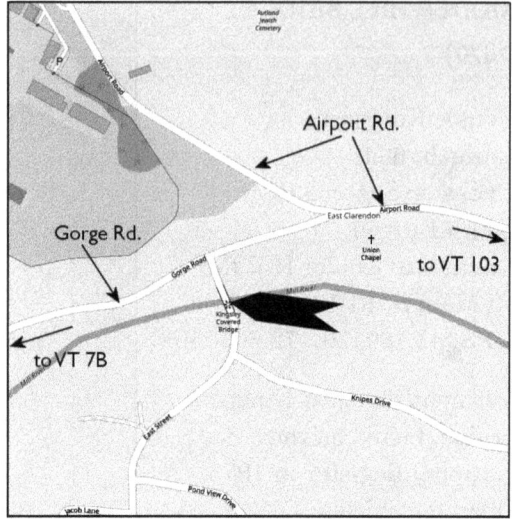

LARKIN BRIDGE (1902)

Truss: Multiple Kingpost
Length: 68 ft
Crosses: First Branch
of White River
Location: Larkin Rd, off Rt
110, Tunbridge
GPS: 43.923018, -72.465443

To meet the angles of the
river crossing, the portals
are slightly skewed, forming
a parallelogram. Listed on
the National Register in
1974. Open to vehicles.

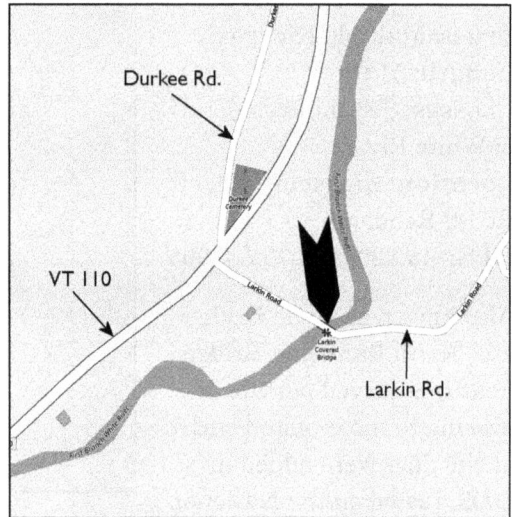

LEDOUX HOMETOWN FOOTBRIDGE (2008)

Truss: Town Lattice
Length: 15 ft
Crosses: unnamed brook
Location: Reading
Elementary School, Rt
106/Main St, Felchville
GPS: 43.452782, -72.535355

Built as a school project by
3rd and 4th grade students,
giving access to town hiking
trails.

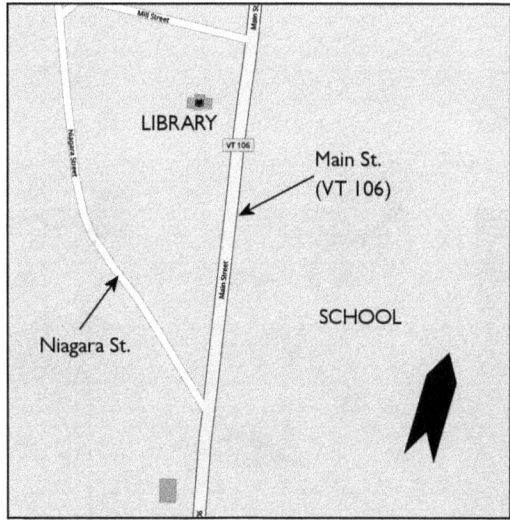

LINCOLN BRIDGE (1877)

Truss: Modified Pratt Truss
with Arch
Length: 136 ft
Crosses: Ottauquechee
River
Location: Fletcher Hill Rd,
off Rt 4/W Woodstock Rd, W
Woodstock
GPS: 43.600577, -72.569001

Named for a local family.
Only known standing
wooden bridge employing the
Pratt Truss. Listed on the
National Register in 1973. Open to vehicles.

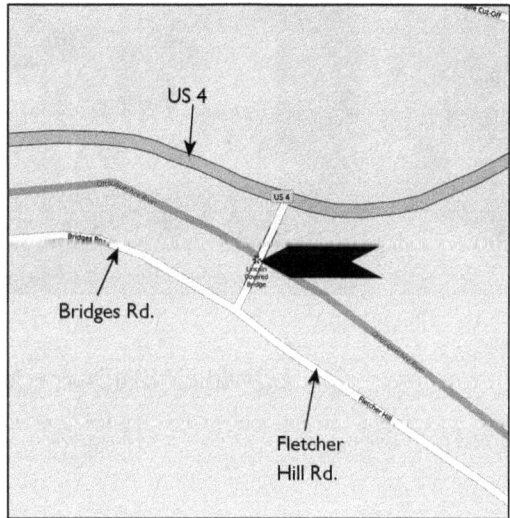

LONGLEY BRIDGE • Montgomery

LONGLEY BRIDGE (1863)

Truss: Town Lattice
Length: 85 ft
Location: Longley Bridge Rd, off North Main St/Rt 118, Montgomery
GPS: 44.907241, -72.655597

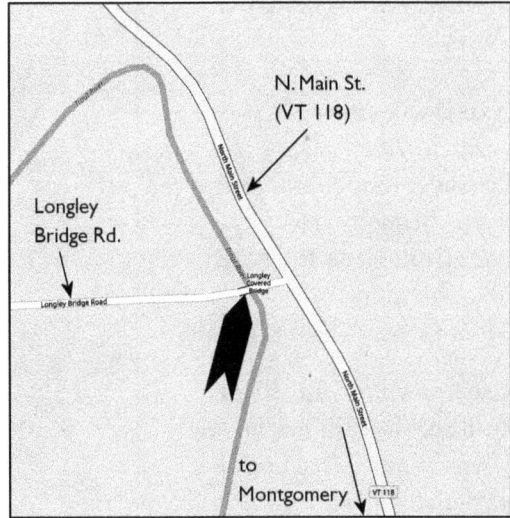

Also known as Harnois Bridge and Head Bridge. The oldest of six surviving bridges built by brothers Sheldon and Savannah Jewett, who operated a sawmill in Montgomery. The others are Comstock, Fuller, Hutchins, Hectorville and West Hill. Listed on the National Register in 1974. Substantially rebuilt, it was reopened to vehicles in 2017.

LORD'S CREEK BRIDGE (1881)

Truss: Paddleford Truss
Length: 50 ft
Crosses: Black River
Location: Covered Bridge Rd, off RT 5 or Rt 58, Irasburg
GPS: 44.816555, -72.266305

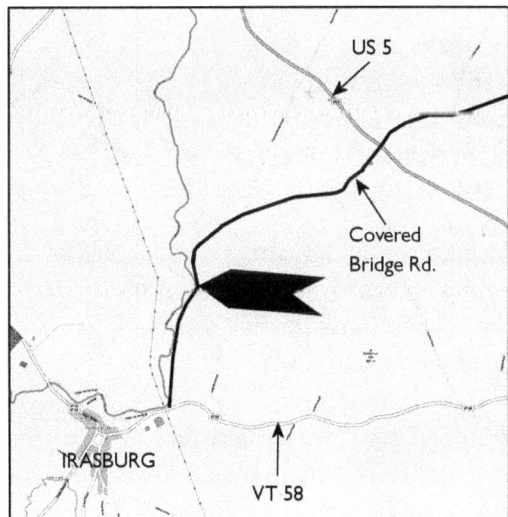

Relocated from Lord's Creek to this farm in 1958. Sides and portals are uncovered. Bridge at farm lane on west side of road. Private.

LUMBER MILL BRIDGE (1895)

Truss: Queenpost
Length: 70 ft
Crosses: Lamoille River, North Branch
Location: Back Rd, off Rt 109, Belvidere
GPS: 44.743645, -72.741498

Also known as Mill Bridge. Ruins of the mill are visible downstream. Listed on the National Register in 1974. Open to vehicles.

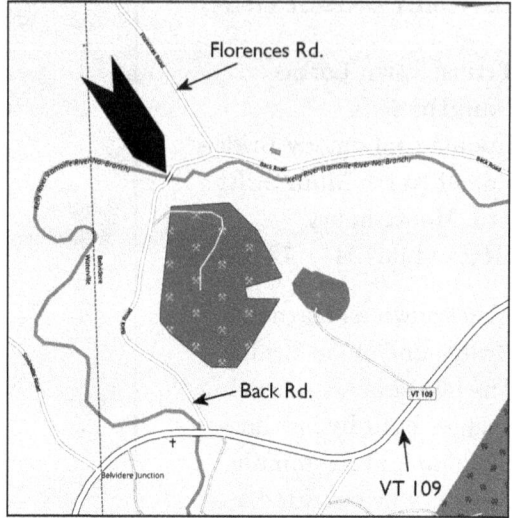

MAPLE STREET BRIDGE (1865)

Truss: Town Lattice
Length: 56 ft
Crosses: Mill Brook
Location: Maple St, off Main St/Rt 104, Fairfax
GPS: 44.663589, -73.010399

Also known as Fairfax Bridge. It was washed onto the brook's bank in the 1927 flood. Some say it was replaced with the ends swapped, and it leans a little as a result. Unusually wide, it accommodates two lanes of traffic. Open to vehicles.

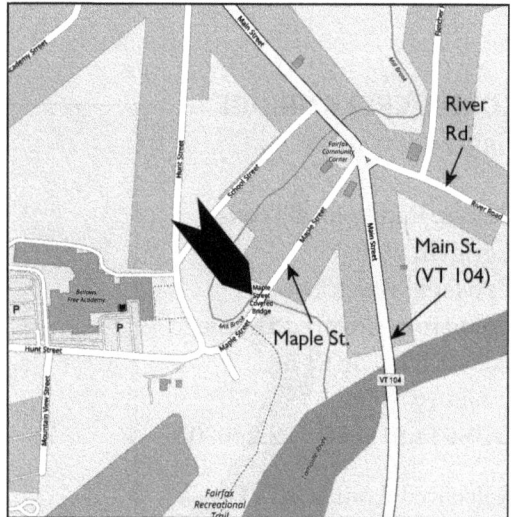

46

MARTIN BRIDGE (1890)

Truss: Queenpost
Length: 45 ft
Crosses: Winooski River
Location: Rt 2, east of
Plainfield
GPS: 44.287542, -72.408191

Named for the original
owner. Also known as Orton
Farm Bridge. The last
remaining covered bridge
built for private farm use.
Listed on the National
Register in 1974. Town has
created a park on south side of road with path leading to the bridge.

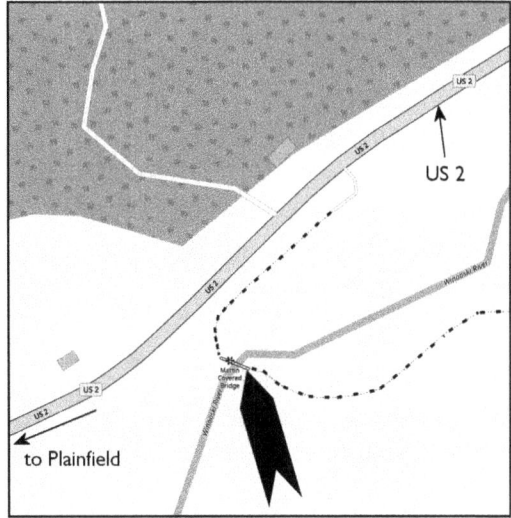

MARTIN'S MILL BRIDGE (1881)

Truss: Town Lattice
Length: 1354 ft
Crosses: Lull's Brook
Location: Martinsville Rd,
off Rt 5, Hartland
GPS: 43.532360, -72.396086

Named for the owner of one
of several mills that were
nearby; some ruins visible.
Also known as Martinsville
Bridge. Listed on the
National Register in 1973. Open to vehicles.

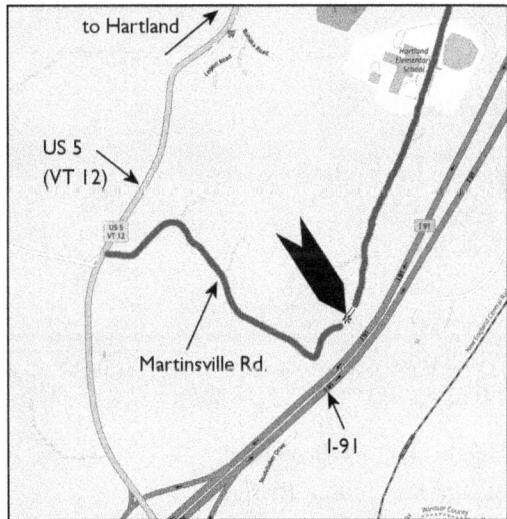

MIDDLE BRIDGE (1969)

Truss: Town Lattice
Length: 139 ft
Crosses: Ottauquechee
River
Location: Mountain Av
(also called Union St), off Rt
4/N Park St, Woodstock
GPS: 43.624673, -72.520385

Also known as Union Street
Bridge. The site of several
covered bridges, succeeded
by an iron bridge in 1877.
When that bridge was
condemned in 1966, it was deemed less expensive to replace it with the
first authentic highway covered bridge built in Vermont since 1895. Open
to vehicles.

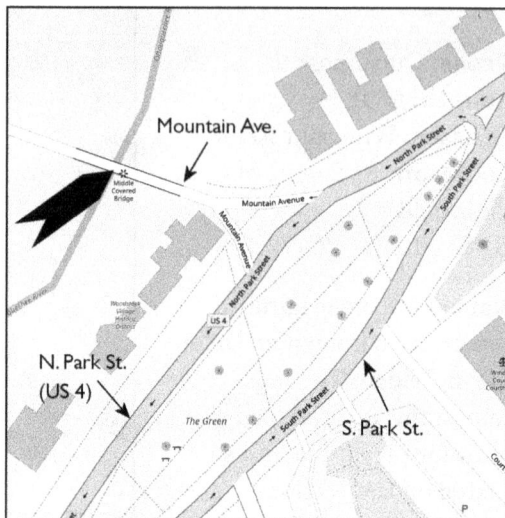

MILL BRIDGE
(TUNBRIDGE) (2000)

Truss: Multiple Kingpost
Length: 73 ft
Crosses: First Branch
of White River
Location: Spring Rd, off Rt
110, Tunbridge
GPS: 43.891769, -72.491552

Also known as Hayward
Bridge and Noble Bridge.
Replica of the 1883 bridge on
this site lost to ice floes in
1999.The historic Hayward and Kibby Mill, which provided lumber for
the 1883 bridge, is adjacent. Open to vehicles.

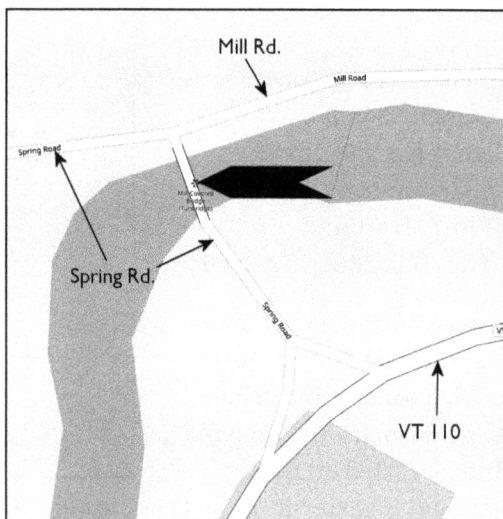

MILLER'S RUN BRIDGE (1878)

Truss: Queenpost
Length: 56
Crosses: Miller's Run
Location: Center St, Off Rt 122/Gilman Rd, Lyndon
GPS: 44.542039, -72.009950

Also known as Bradley Bridge. Listed on the National Register in 1977. Open to vehicles despite truck damage in 2019 and 2020. Parking area with path to the bridge's covered walkway, which was added in 1995.

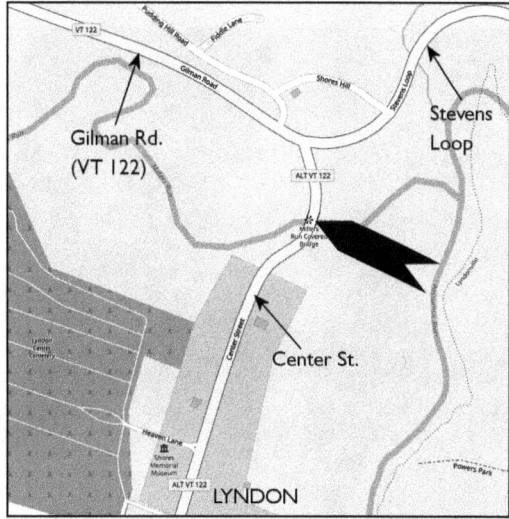

MONTGOMERY BRIDGE (1887)

Truss: Queenpost
Length: 71 ft
Crosses: Lamoille River, North Branch
Location: Montgomery Rd, off Rt 109, Waterville
GPS: 44.705730, -72.760267

Now named for the farmer who, in 1969, climbed on the roof to shovel snow after five feet fell. Also known as Potter Bridge, Listed on the National Register in 1974. Open to vehicles.

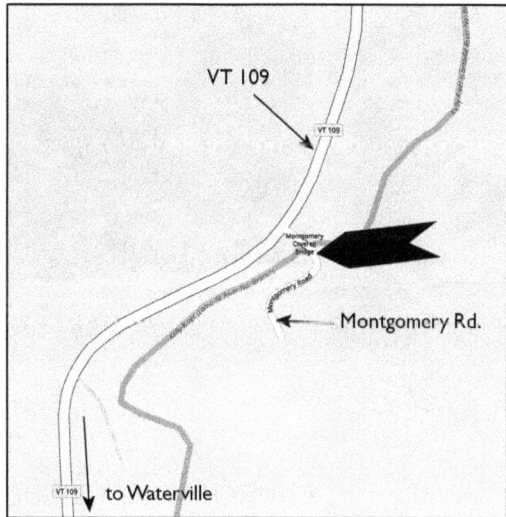

CHURCH STREET BRIDGE • Waterville

MORGAN BRIDGE (1887)

Truss: Queenpost
Length: 71 ft
Crosses: Lamoille River,
North Branch
Location: Morgan Bridge
Rd, between Back Rd and Rt
109, Belvidere
GPS: 44.743481, -72.728035

Named for the farm family
which owned adjacent land.
Construction incorporates
Kingpost trusses within the
Queenpost. Listed on the
National Register in 1974. Open to vehicles.

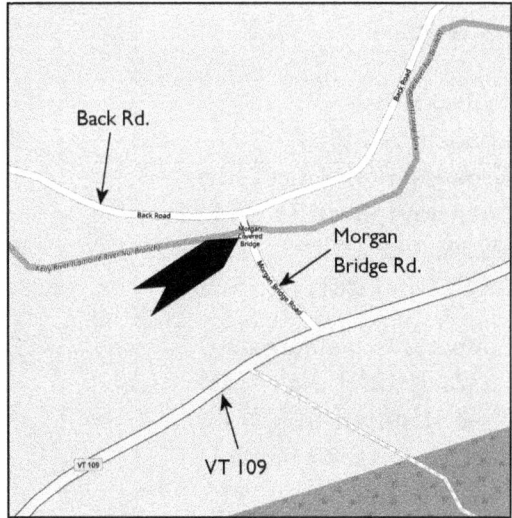

MOSELEY BRIDGE (1899)

Truss: Kingpost
Length: 37 ft
Location: Stony Brook Rd,
off Rt 12A, Northfield
GPS: 44.120362, -72.689181

Named for its builder. Also
known as Stony Brook
Bridge. Painted barn red
inside and out. Listed on the
National Register in 1974.
Open to vehicles.

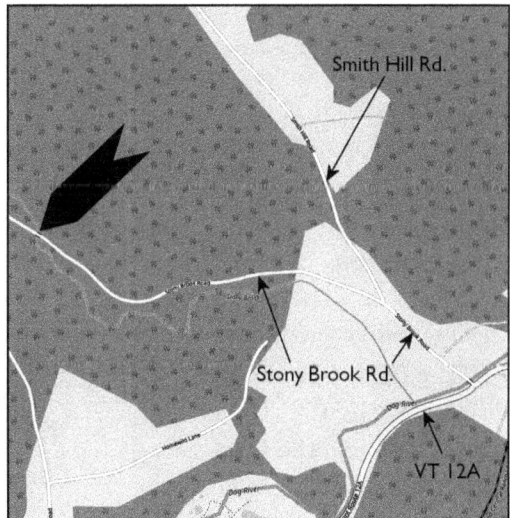

MOUNT ORNE BRIDGE (1911)

Truss: Howe
Length: 267 ft
Crosses: Connecticut River
Location: River Rd, off Rt 2, Lunenburg
GPS: 44.460231, -71.652792

Connects Lunenburg to Lancaster, NH. Named for Orne Mountain in Lancaster. Listed on the National Register in 1976. Open to vehicles.

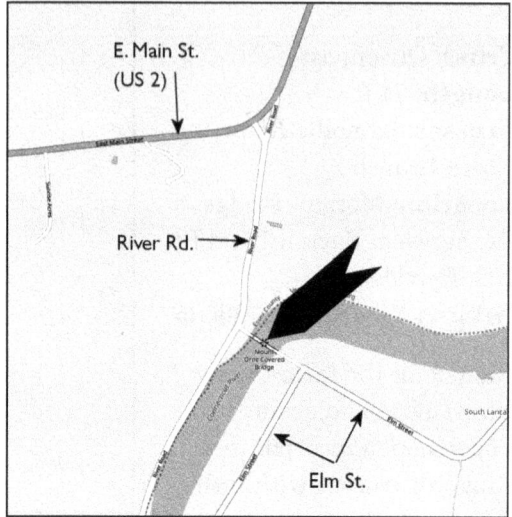

MOXLEY BRIDGE (1883)

Truss: Queenpost
Length: 56 ft
Crosses: First Branch of White River
Location: Moxley Rd, off Rt 110, Chelsea
GPS: 43.956963, -72.463386

Also known as Guy Bridge. Like the Larkin Bridge, the portals are slightly skewed due to the angle the road crosses the river. Listed on the National Register in 1974 Open to vehicles.

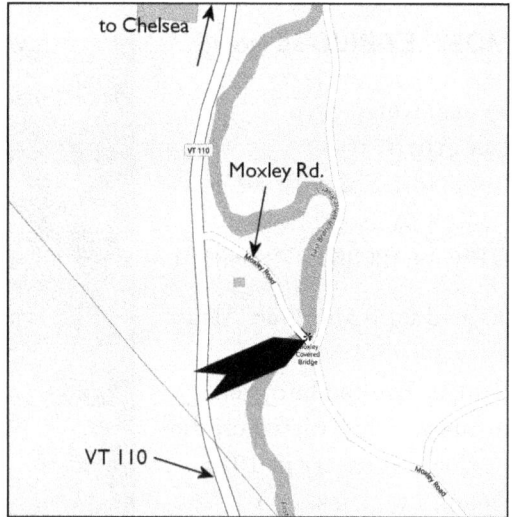

ORNE BRIDGE (1999)

Truss: Paddleford
Length: 87 ft
Crosses: Black River
Location: Covered Bridge
Rd, Coventry (also called
Back Coventry Rd, Irasburg)
GPS: 44.860854, -72.273427

Also known as Black River
Bridge, Coventry Bridge and
Irasburg Bridge. Largely a
replica of an 1881 bridge
destroyed by arson in 1997.
Both the original and replica
were built with a 14-panel Paddleford truss, representing Vermont's 14
counties and status as the 14th state. Open to vehicles.

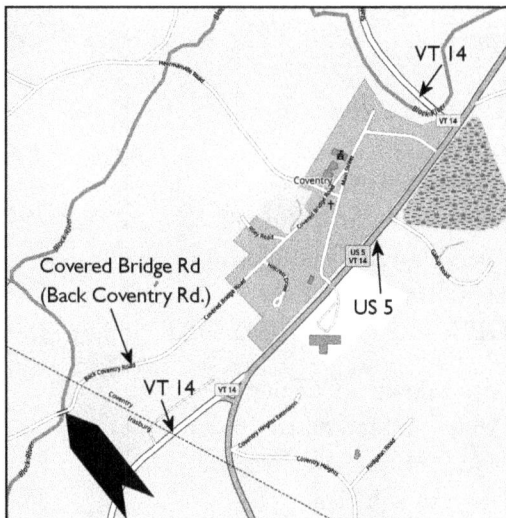

PAPER MILL BRIDGE (BENNINGTON) (1889)

Truss: Town Lattice
Length: 125 ft
Crosses: Walloomsac River
Location: Murphy Rd, south
of N Bennington Rd/Rt 67A,
Bennington
GPS: 42.912742, -73.233412

Also known as Paper Mill
Village Bridge and
Bennington Falls Bridge, the
latter for the former name of
the adjacent dam. Listed on the National Register in 1973. Completely
rebuilt in 2000. Open to vehicles.

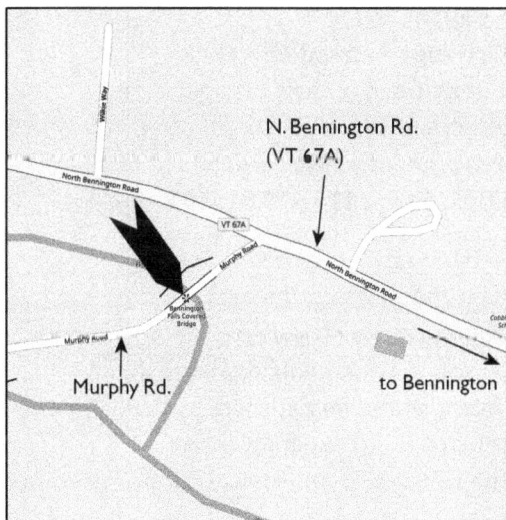

PINE BROOK BRIDGE (1872)

Truss: Kingpost
Length: 48 ft
Crosses: Pine Brook
Location: North Rd, off Tremblay Rd, east of Main St/Rt 100, Waitsfield
GPS: 44.205685, -72.792083

Also known as Wilder Bridge. Listed on the National Register in 1974. Open to vehicles.

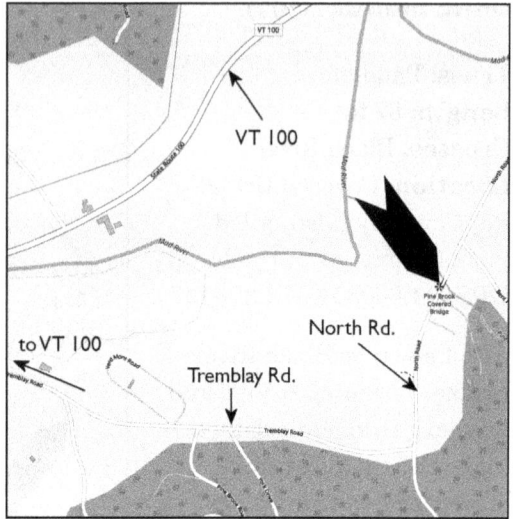

POLAND BRIDGE (1887)

Truss: Burr Arch
Length: 153 ft
Crosses: Lamoille River
Location: Cambridge Junction Rd, off Rt 15, Jeffersonville (Cambridge)
GPS: 44.651115, -72.814594

Named for the retired judge who championed the bridge to give northern villages access to the Cambridge Junction railway station, a controversial expenditure at the time. Also known as Cambridge Junction Bridge, Station Bridge and Kissing Bridge. Listed on the National Register in 1974. Open to vehicles. Access point for Lamoille Valley Rail Trail.

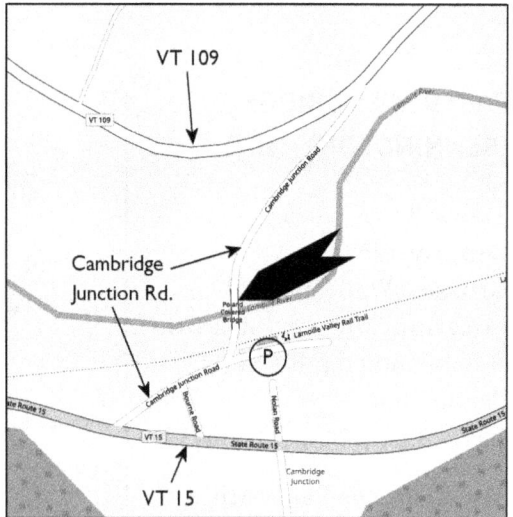

POWER HOUSE BRIDGE (1872)

Truss: Queenpost
Length: 63 ft
Crosses: Gihon River
Location: School St, off Rt 100C, Johnson
GPS: 44.636095, -72.670392

Named for a former hydroelectric station. Also known as Johnson Bridge and School Street Bridge. Crushed by snow in 2001, it was rebuilt in 2002. Park with waterfalls and swimming hole adjacent. Listed on the National Register in 1974. Open to vehicles.

PULP MILL BRIDGE (1853)

Truss: King Post with Burr Arch
Length: 199 ft
Crosses: Otter Creek
Location: Pulp Mill Bridge Rd, off Rt 23/Weybridge Rd, Middlebury
GPS: 44.024647, -73.177495

Also known as Paper Mill Bridge. Said to be Vermont's oldest covered bridge. Unverified claims date it to 1820 or earlier, but an expert who studied the bridge and its history believes it was built in the 1850s. One of two double-barreled (two-lane) bridges in the state. Open to vehicles. Pedestrian walkway with views of waterfall.

POWER HOUSE BRIDGE • Johnson

HAMMOND BRIDGE • Pittsford

QUECHEE BRIDGE (1970)

Romantic Shelter
Crosses: Ottauquechee River
Length: 70 ft
Location: Waterman Hill Rd
between Rt 4/Woodstock Rd
and Quechee Main St,
Quechee
GPS: 43.645464, -72.418884

Open to vehicles; pedestrian
walkway.

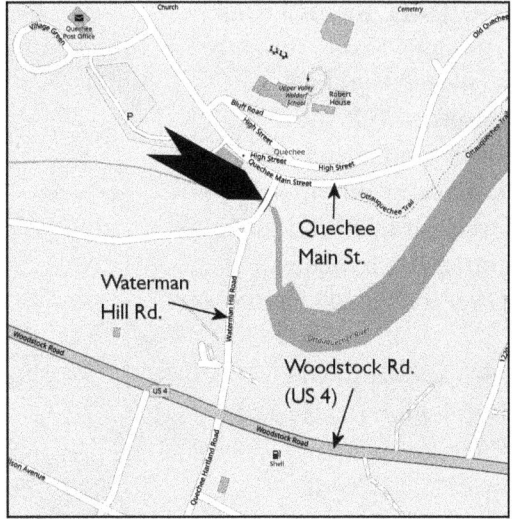

QUINLAN BRIDGE (1849)

Truss: Burr Arch
Length: 86 ft
Crosses: Lewis Creek
Location: Monkton Rd at
Spear St, east of Rt 7,
Charlotte
GPS: 44.276318, -73.183780

Also known as Sherman
Bridge and Lower Bridge.
Listed on the National
Register in 1974.

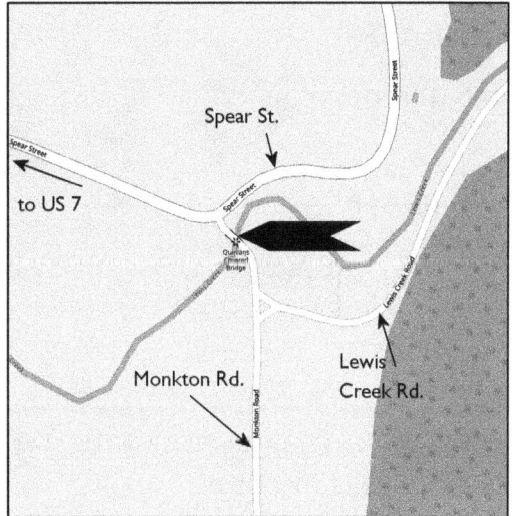

RANDALL BRIDGE (1865)

Truss: Queen Post
Length: 68 ft
Crosses: Passumpsic River
Location: Burrington
Bridge Rd, off Rt 114/E
Burke Rd, Lyndon
GPS: 44.553522, -71.969528

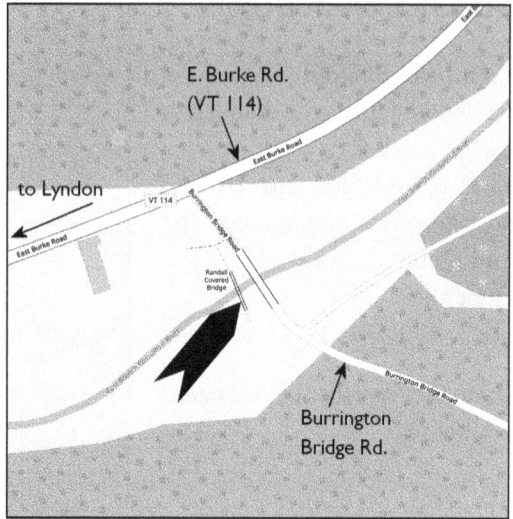

Also known as Old
Burrington Bridge and
Burrington Bridge. Bypassed
in 1965, bridge is
immediately upstream of the
re-routed road. Listed on the National Register in 1974. Open to
pedestrians.

RED BRIDGE (1896)

Truss: Queenpost
Length: 64 ft
Crosses: Sterling Brook
Location: Cole Hill Rd, off
Sterling Valley Rd, west of
Stagecoach Rd, Morristown
GPS: 44.518604, -72.677767

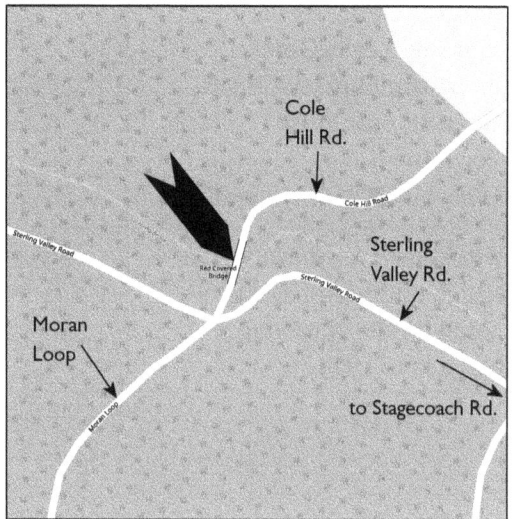

Also known as Chaffee
Bridge and Sterling Brook
Bridge. Painted barn red,
and built with Kingpost
truss within the Queenpost
truss. Listed on the National
Register in 1974. Open to vehicles.

RIVER ROAD BRIDGE (1910)

Truss: Town Lattice
Length: 94 ft
Crosses: Missisquoi River
Location: Veilleux Rd, between Rt 101 and River Rd, Troy
GPS: 44.956376, -72.393453

The bridge was destroyed on February 6, 2021 when a snowmobile passing through it caught fire. The fire spread to the bridge, which collapsed into the river. The possibility of replacing the bridge with a replica is under discussion in the town. Also known as School Bridge or School House Bridge, it was near but not on River Road. It was the most northerly covered bridge in Vermont.

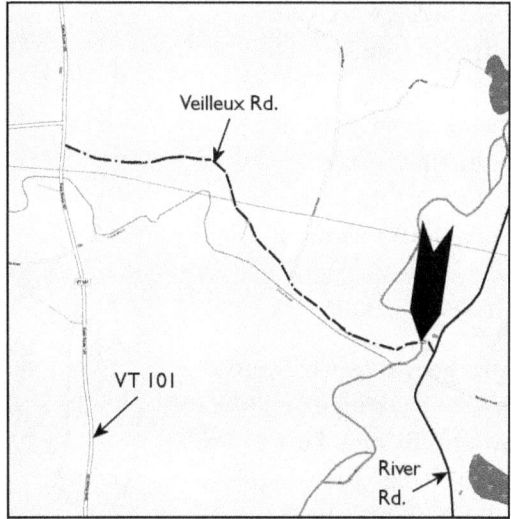

ROBBINS NEST BRIDGE (1962)

Truss: Queenpost
Length: 57 ft
Crosses: Jail Branch, Winooski River
Location: Rt 302, 1.7 mi N of roundabout, Barre
GPS: 44.178700, -72.470783

Built by Robert Robbins is a replica of a bridge that stood downstream and was swept away in the 1927 flood.
Visible on south side of road. Private.

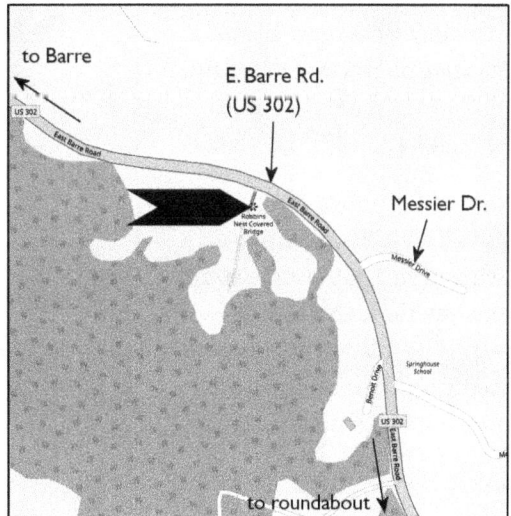

SALISBURY STATION BRIDGE (1865)

Truss: Town Lattice
Length: 153 ft
Crosses: Otter Creek
Location: Swamp Rd, off Rt 30, Cornwall
GPS: 43.918085, -73.173969

Also known as Cornwall-Salisbury Bridge and Cedar Swamp Bridge. Lost to fire in 2016. The town hopes to rebuild it, but there was no announced plan at press time.

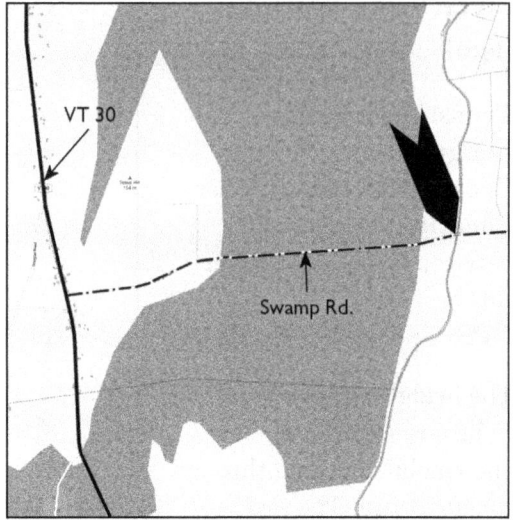

SALMOND BRIDGE (1875)

Truss: Multiple King Post
Length: 53 ft
Crosses: Sherman Brook
Location: Henry Gould Rd, off Rt 131, Weathersfield
GPS: 43.426927, -72.488247

Named for a local family. Moved from its original location in 1959 due to dam construction, the bridge served as a town storage shed until being relocated in 1986. Open to pedestrians.

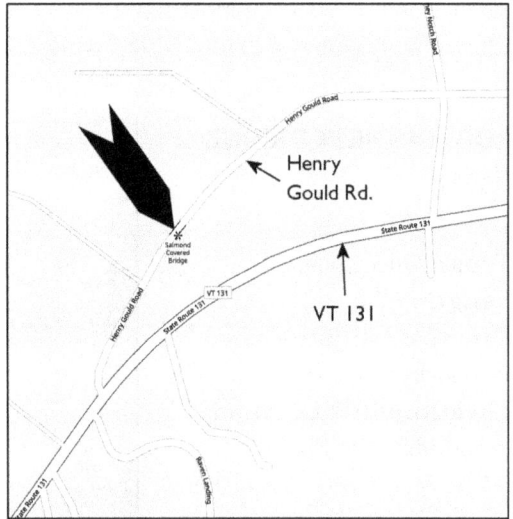

SANBORN BRIDGE (1867)

Truss: Paddleford
Length: 118
Crosses: Passumpsic River
Location: On W side of Rt 5/Main St, just S of 114/122 jct, Lyndonville
GPS: 44.544090, -72.000882

Also known as Centre Bridge. Originally carrying a road on the Sanborn farm, it was relocated to the Lynburke Motel property in 1960. Listed on the National Register in 1974. Motel is closed. At press time the bridge is unsafe for pedestrians.

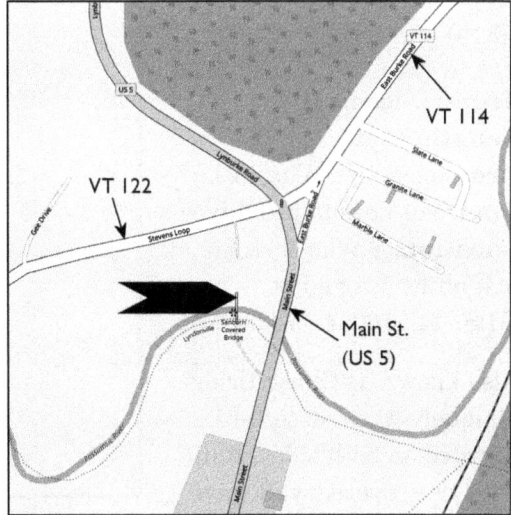

SANDERSON BRIDGE (1838)

Truss: Town Lattice
Length: 132 ft
Crosses: Otter Creek
Location: Pearl St, off Rt 7, Brandon
GPS: 43.789579, -73.111657

Substantially rebuilt in 2003. Listed on the National Register in 1974. Open to vehicles.

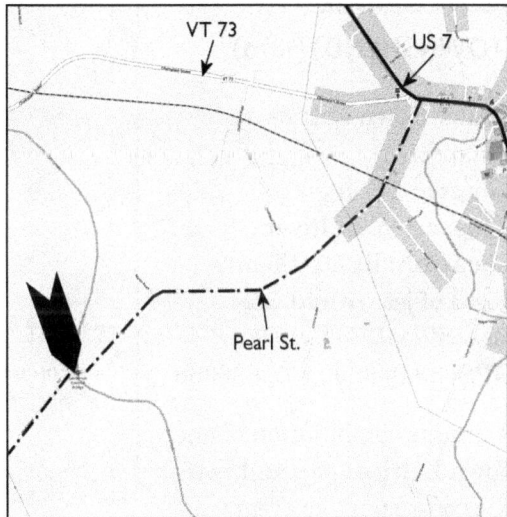

SCHOOLHOUSE BRIDGE (1879)

Truss: Queenpost
Length: 42 ft
Crosses: South Wheelock
Branch of Passumpsic River
Location: S Wheelock Rd,
just off Rt 5, Lyndon
GPS: 44.516054, -72.009761

Also known as Chase Bridge.
Uniquely, the trusses are
boarded on both sides. Built
with two covered walkways

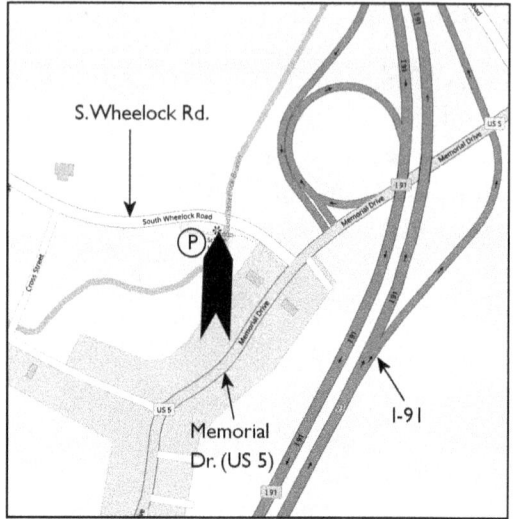

of which one remains. The first Vermont bridge to be listed on the
National Register, in 1971. Bypassed that year, it is open to pedestrians.
Parking area on south side of road.

SCOTT BRIDGE (TOWNSHEND) (1870)

Truss: Town Lattice and
Kingpost
Length: 277 ft
Crosses: West River
Location: Rt 30, 1.5 mi
north of jct with Rt 35,
Townshend
GPS: 43.048690, -72.696366

A unique combination of one
Town Lattice span and two
Kingpost spans to create

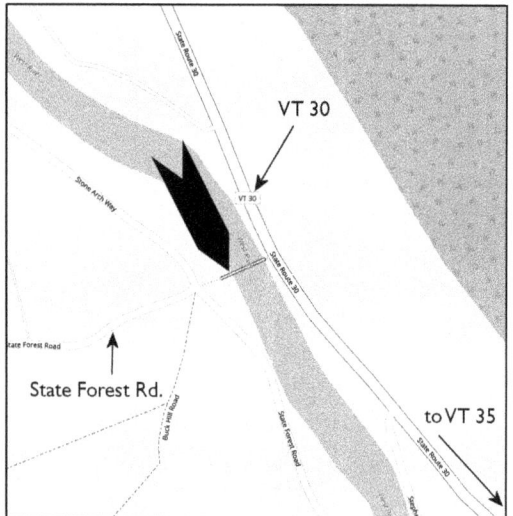

perhaps the longest covered bridge entirely in Vermont (see West
Dummerston Bridge). The Town Lattice portion is the longest wooden

span in Vermont. Closed to traffic in 1955. Listed on the National Register in 1973. Open to pedestrians.

SCRIBNER BRIDGE (1919)

Truss: Queenpost
Length: 48 ft
Crosses: Gihon River
Location: Rocky Rd, off Rt 100C, Johnson
GPS: 44.638175, -72.648495

Rocky Road was washed out in the 2019 Halloween flood, and it is unknown at this printing when access to the bridge will be restored. Also known as DeGoosh Bridge and Mudget Bridge.

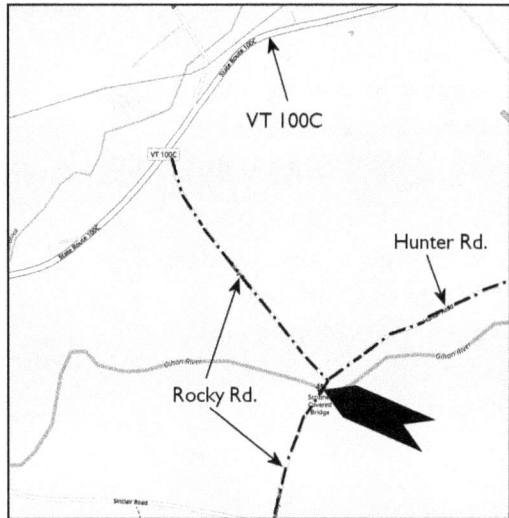

SECOND BRIDGE (1872)

Truss: Queenpost
Length: 57 ft
Crosses: Cox Brook
Location: Cox Brook Rd, off Rt 12, Northfield Falls
GPS: 44.172766, -72.653068

Also known as Newell Bridge and Lower Cox Brook Bridge. One of three covered bridges on this road, all painted barn red. This and Station Bridge are the only covered bridges in Vermont that can be viewed from the other. Listed on the National Register in 1974. Open to vehicles.

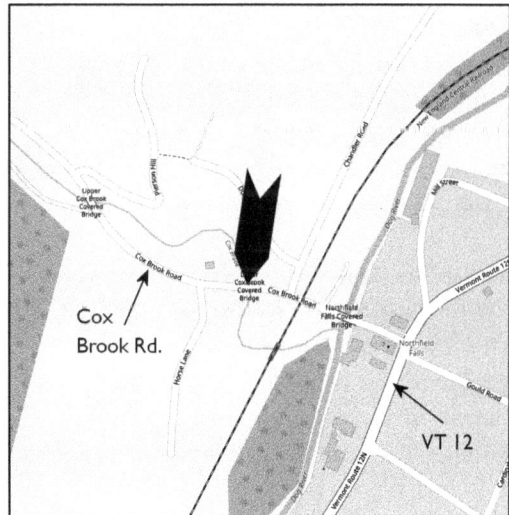

SEGUIN BRIDGE (1849)

Truss: Burr Arch
Length: 71 ft
Crosses: Lewis Creek
Location: Roscoe Rd, off
Prindle Rd, Charlotte
GPS: 44.288988, -73.150166

Named for a local family.
Also known as Upper Bridge.
Listed on the National
Register in 1974 where it
was misspelled Sequin.
Open to vehicles.

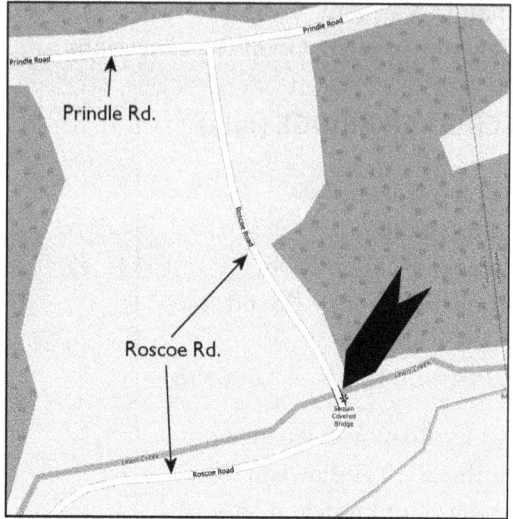

SHELBURNE MUSEUM
BRIDGE (1845)

Truss: Burr Arch
Length: 186 ft
Crosses: Burr Pond
Location: Ethan Allen
Hwy/Shelburne Rd,
Shelburne
GPS: 44.376934, -73.229480

Originally located in
Cambridge, so also known as
Cambridge Bridge. One of
Vermont's two "double
barrel" or two-lane covered
bridges. Open to pedestrians on museum grounds.

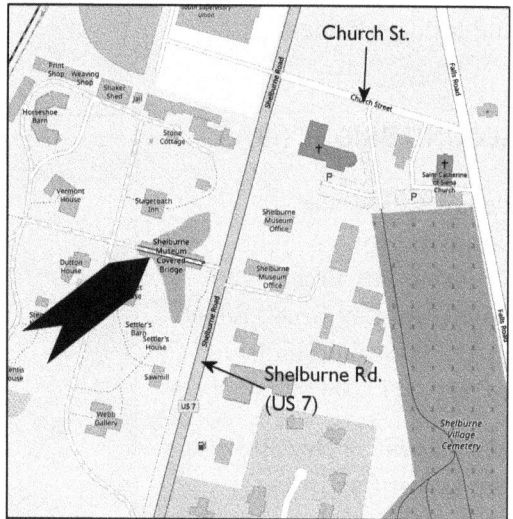

SHOREHAM RAILROAD BRIDGE (1897)

Truss: Howe Truss
Length: 109 feet
Crosses: Lemon Fair River
Location: intersection of
Dame Rd and Shoreham
Depot Rd, Shoreham
GPS: 43.859305, -73.255976

Also known as East
Shoreham Bridge and
Rutland Railroad Bridge.
One of two covered railroad
bridges remaining in Vermont, built by the Rutland Railroad Co. Last
used in 1951, the tracks are now gone. A wooden deck laid atop railroad
ties permits foot traffic. Park at fishing access point. Listed on the
National Register in 1974.

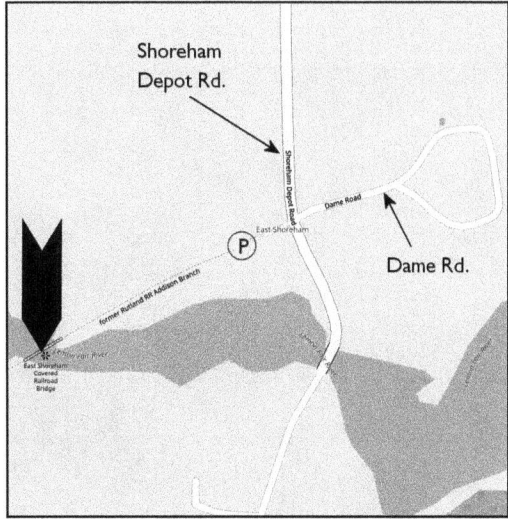

SILK BRIDGE (1840)

Truss: Town Lattice
Length: 88 ft
Crosses: Walloomsac River
Location: Silk Rd, south of
N Bennington Rd/Rt 67A,
Bennington
GPS: 42.909396, -73.225357

Silk was a local family
name. Also known as Locust
Grove Bridge and Robinson
Bridge. Listed on the
National Register in 1973. Repaired after suffering damage resulting
from Hurricane Irene in 2011. Open to vehicles.

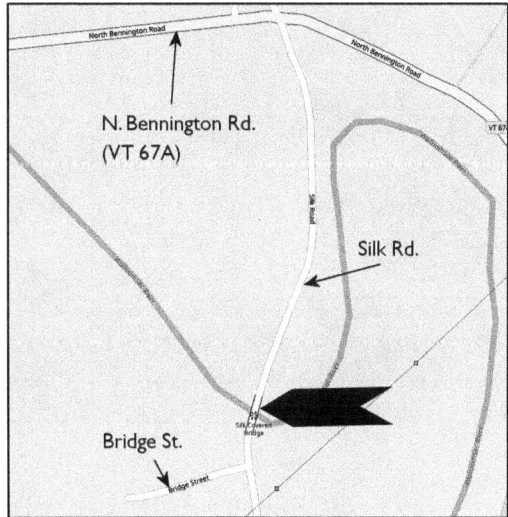

SHOREHAM RAILROAD BRIDGE • Shoreham

SLAUGHTER HOUSE BRIDGE (1872)

Truss: Queenpost
Length: 60 ft
Crosses: Dog River
Location: Slaughterhouse Rd, off Rt 12, Northfield Falls
GPS: 44.168531, -72.654659

Barn red with rounded portals. Listed on the National Register in 1974. Open to vehicles.

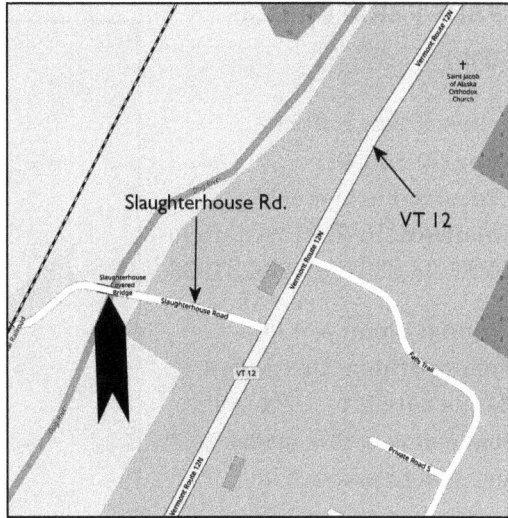

SNOW BRIDGE (1997)

Romantic Shelter
Crosses: ski trail
Length: 50 ft
Location: Snowbridge Rd, Stratton Mountain
GPS: 43.111117, -72.916672

Open to vehicles.

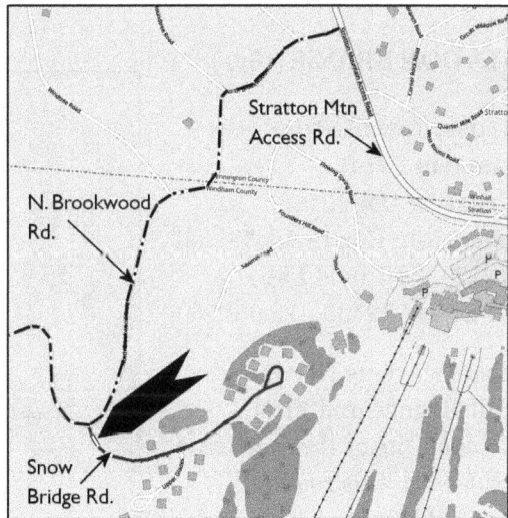

SPADE FARM BRIDGE (1850)

Truss: Town Lattice
Length: 85 feet
Crosses: Farm creek
Location: Rt 7, Ferrisburgh
GPS: 44.237458, -73.231963

Original name was Old Hollow Bridge. Unverified claims date it to 1824. Sam Spade moved this bridge to his farm to prevent its destruction in the 1950s. Now on grounds of the Vermont Flannel Company store. Open to pedestrians.

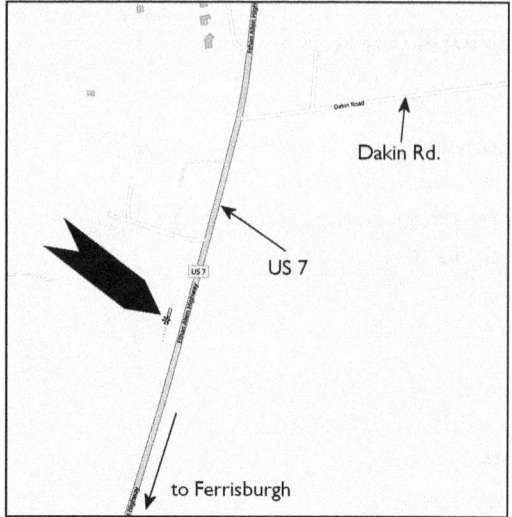

STATION BRIDGE (1872)

Truss: Town Lattice
Length: 137 ft
Crosses: Dog River
Location: Cox Brook Rd, off Rt 12, Northfield Falls
GPS: 44.172435, -72.651560

Also known as Northfield Falls Bridge and First Bridge. One of three covered bridges on this road, all painted barn red. This and Second Bridge are the only covered bridges in Vermont that can be viewed from the other. Railfans will enjoy views of active New England Central Railroad tracks. Listed on the National Register in 1974. Open to vehicles.

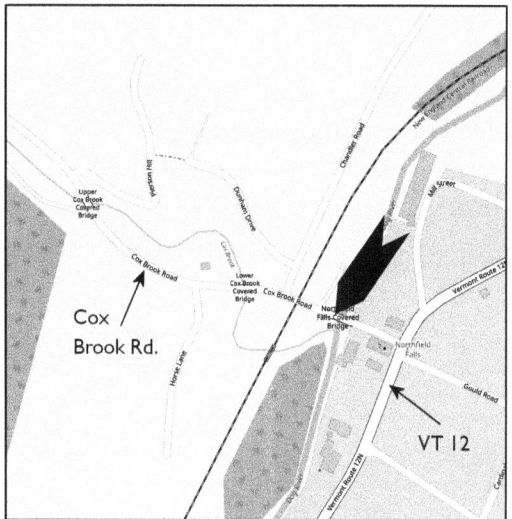

STOWE WALKWAY
BRIDGE (1973)

Romantic Shelter
Crosses: West Branch,
Waterbury River (aka West
Branch, Little River)
Length: 150 ft
Location: Rt 108/Mountain
Rd, off Rt 100, Stowe
GPS: 44.466438, -72.688023

Provides pedestrian access
along Rt 108 through the
village. Rebuilt 2015.

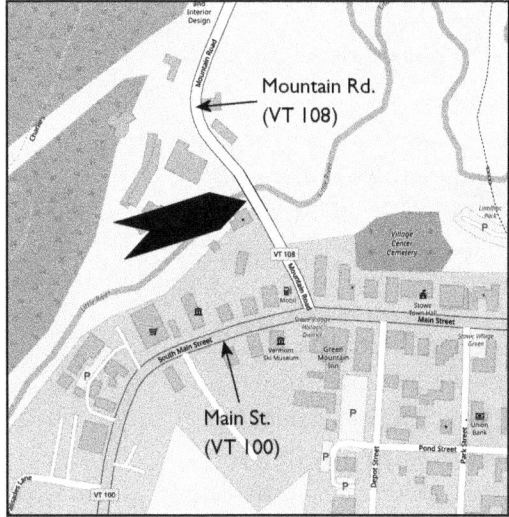

TAFTSVILLE BRIDGE (1836)

Truss: Multiple King Post
and arch
Length: 189 ft
Crosses: Ottauquechee
River
Location: Covered Bridge
Rd, off Rt 4/Woodstock Rd,
Woodstock
GPS: 43.630986, -72.467848

Named for the locality. One
of Vermont's oldest covered
bridges, it features an
unusual construction of
laminated arches that were added to the kingpost's trusses early in the
20th century. Damaged by Hurricane Irene's flooding in 2011, it was
reopened in 2013. Set in a gorge below the historic powerhouse dam.
Listed on the National Register in 1973. Open to vehicles.

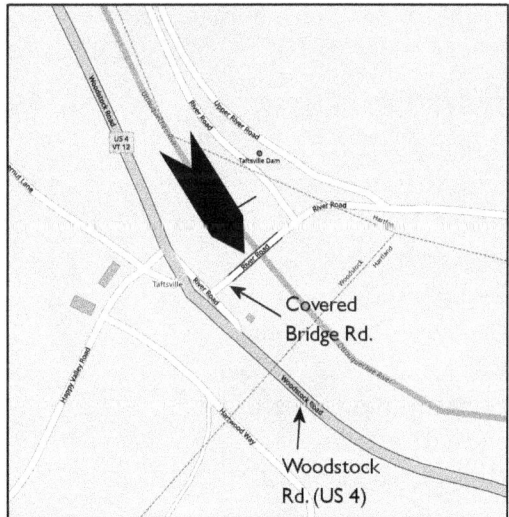

TEAGO BRIDGE (1870)

Truss: Town Lattice
Length: 39 ft
Crosses: Barnard Brook
Location: Farm lane off
Pomfret Rd, off Rt 12,
Woodstock
GPS: 43.659736, -72.534264

Named for its locality, also
known as Smith Bridge and
South Pomfret Bridge. A
bridge originally in Hyde
Park was no longer needed.
It was removed, purchased and cut in half in 1973. The other half was
known as Twigg-Smith Bridge and was located in West Windsor until
being destroyed by a wind storm in 2001. Teago Bridge is the other half.
Visible on west side of road. Private.

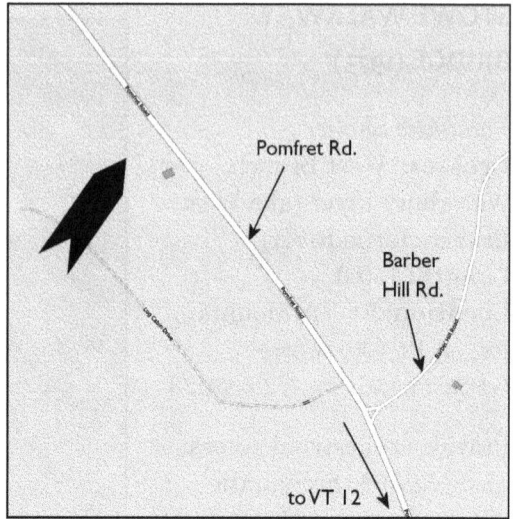

THETFORD CENTER

BRIDGE (1857)

Truss: Haupt Truss variant
with arch
Length: 129 ft
Crosses: Ompompanoosuc
River
Location: Tucker Hill Rd,
off Rt 113, Thetford
GPS: 43.832032, -72.252745

Also known as Sayres Bridge.
Vermont's only Haupt Truss
bridge. Date of construction is unknown. Some sources say the bridge was
built in 1839, but that is the year Haupt patented his truss design. Two

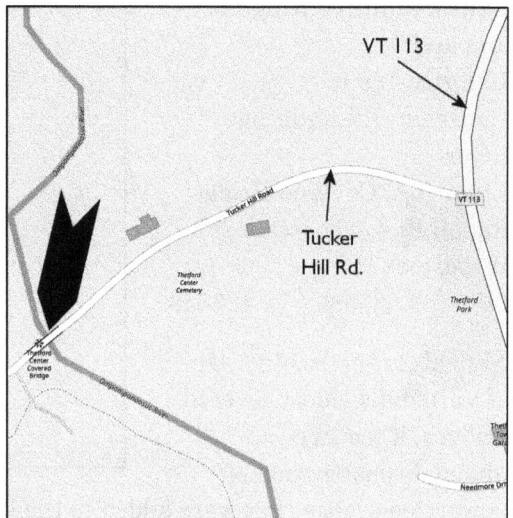

Pennsylvania bridges using it were built in 1854; the other bridge in Thetford was built in 1857, so we are choosing that as the date. The builder may not actually have been familiar with the Haupt Truss and built this apparent variant by chance. Listed on the National Register in 1974. Open to vehicles.

THIRD BRIDGE (1872)

Truss: Queenpost
Length: 52 ft
Crosses: Cox Brook
Location: Cox Brook Rd, off Rt 12, Northfield Falls
GPS: 44.173737, -72.655580

Also known as Upper Cox Brook Bridge. One of three covered bridges on this road, all painted barn red. Listed on the National Register in 1974. Open to vehicles.

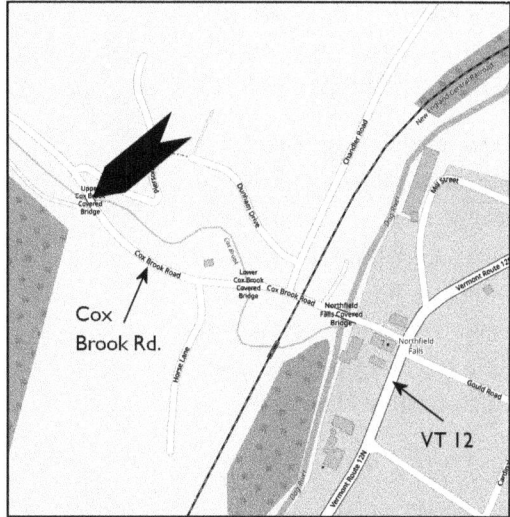

TITCOMB BRIDGE (1880)

Truss: Multiple King Post
Length: 48
Crosses: Schoolhouse Brook
Location: farm lane east off Rt 106, south of Maple St, Weathersfield
GPS: 43.367463, -72.516173

Originally known as Stoughton Bridge, it was moved in 1959 due to construction of a dam and restored in 1963 on the Titcomb Farm. As of press time, the Titcomb family welcome visitors to the bridge.

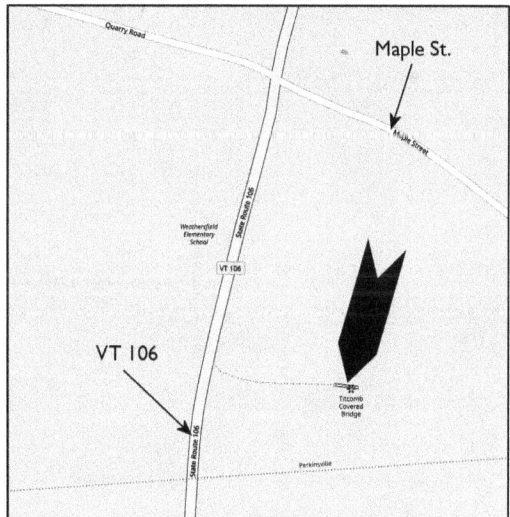

TWIN BRIDGE (1850)

Truss: Town Lattice
Length: 64 ft
Crosses: n/a
Location: E Pittsford Rd, off
Rt 7, Rutland
GPS: 43.648650, -72.972731

Originally one of two bridges
over East Creek that were
swept downstream in 1947
when Chittenden Reservoir
burst its dam. Only this one
was saved, and now serves
as a town equipment shed
just south of the creek.

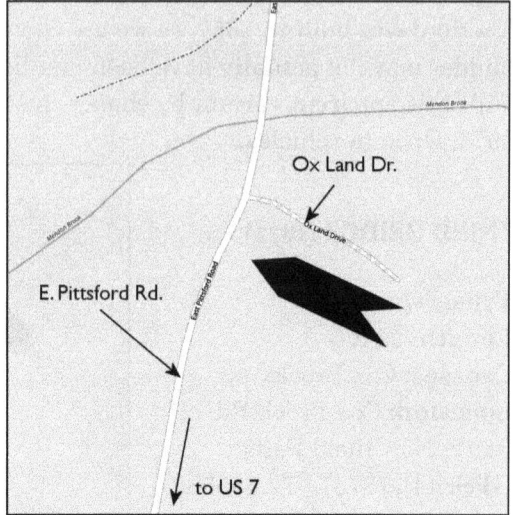

UNION VILLAGE BRIDGE (1867)

Truss: Multiple Kingpost
with Arch
Length: 113 ft
Crosses: Ompompanoosuc
River
Location: Academy Rd, off
Rt 132, Thetford
GPS: 43.788642, -72.254039

Adjacent to Union Village
Dam Recreation Area, Listed
on the National Register in
1974.Open to vehicles.

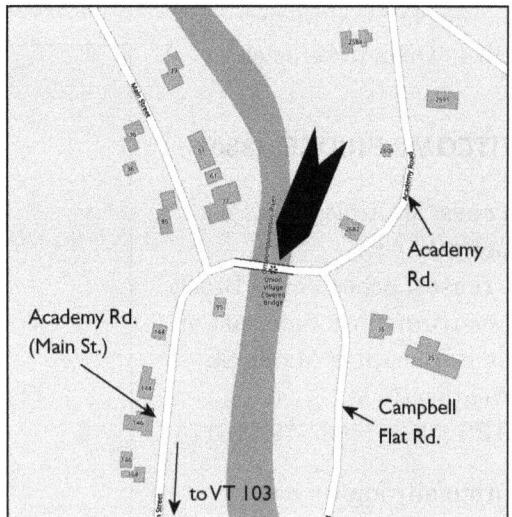

UPPER FALLS BRIDGE (1840)

Truss: Town Lattice
Length: 120 ft
Crosses: Black River
Location: Upper Falls Rd, off Rt 131, Weathersfield
GPS: 43.398687, -72.522072

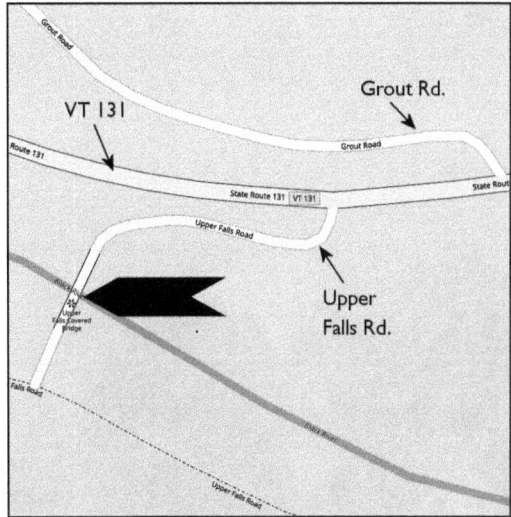

Also known as Downers Bridge after the section of Weathersfield. Its portals feature unique Greek Revival elements. Ruins of a millworks are visible upstream. Listed on the National Register in 1973. Open to vehicles.

VICTORIAN VILLAGE BRIDGE (1872/1967)

Truss: Modified King Post
Length: 44 ft
Crosses: Rock Brook
Location: Grounds of Vermont Country Store, Rockingham Rd/Rt 103, Rockingham
GPS: 43.196875, -72.504166

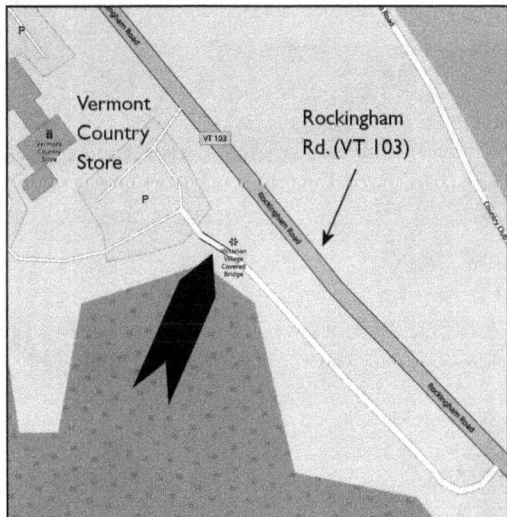

Originally the Depot Bridge in Townshend, it was dismantled in 1959 to make way for a dam. Saved from destruction by Vermont Country Store founder Vrest Orton, a shortened version of the bridge was reassembled at the store's location in Rockingham in 1967. Origin of the name is not known. The store refers to it as their "Kissing Bridge."

WARREN BRIDGE • Warren

VILLAGE BRIDGE (WAITSFIELD) (1833)

Truss: Burr Arch
Length: 105 ft
Crosses: Mad River
Location: Bridge St, off Main St/Rt 100, Waitsfield
GPS: 44.189350, -72.823528

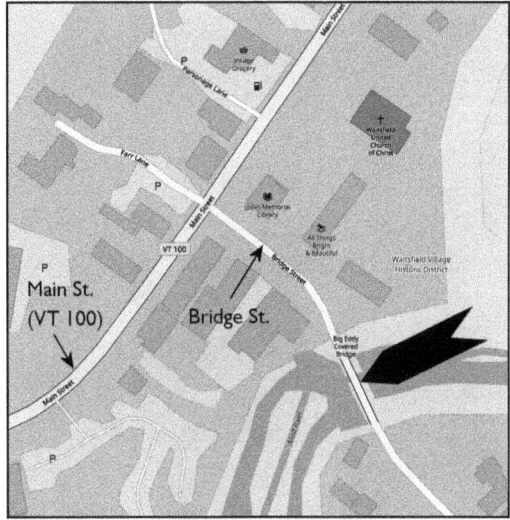

Also known as Waitsfield Bridge. Great Eddy Bridge and Big Eddy Bridge. At least the second oldest Vermont covered bridge if not the oldest (see Pulp Mill Bridge). A walkway with views of the eddy was added in 1940. The bridge was pummeled by Hurricane Irene's flood waters in 2011, but survived. Listed on the National Register in 1974. Open to vehicles.

WARREN BRIDGE (1880)

Truss: Queenpost
Length: 58 ft
Crosses: Mad River
Location: Covered Bridge Rd, off Main St, Warren
GPS: 44.111119, -72.857024

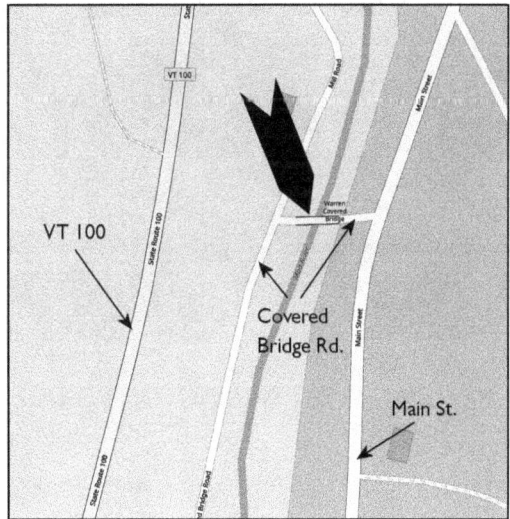

Also known as Lincoln Gap Bridge. Like the Schoolhouse Bridge, the truss is covered inside and out. Listed on the National Register in 1974. Open to vehicles.

WEST ARLINGTON BRIDGE • West Arlington

WEST ARLINGTON BRIDGE (1852)

Truss: Town Lattice
Length: 84 ft
Crosses: Batten Kill (aka Battenkill River)
Location: Covered Bridge Rd, south of Batten Kill Rd/Rt 313, West Arlington
GPS: 43.104289, -73.220352

Also known as Arlington Bridge and Bridge at the Green. One of the most photographed bridges, with well-known swimming hole below.

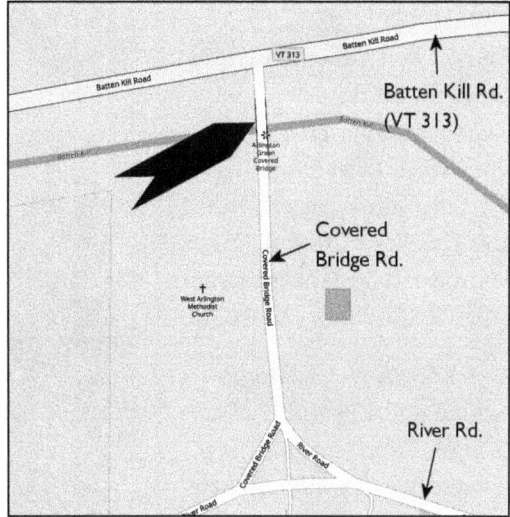

WEST DUMMERSTON BRIDGE (1872)

Truss: Town Lattice
Length: 277 ft
Crosses: West River
Location: East West Rd, between West River Rd/Rt 30 and Camp Arden Rd, West Dummerston
GPS: 42.936649, -72.612911

A two-span bridge, perhaps the longest entirely in Vermont (see Scott Bridge). Popular swimming hole below. Listed on the National Register in 1973. Open to vehicles.

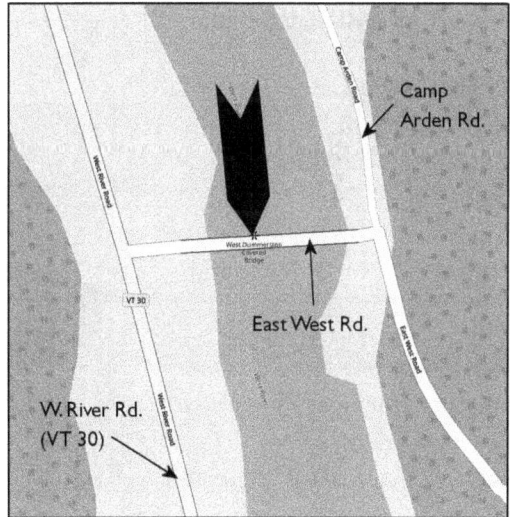

WEST HILL BRIDGE (1883)

Truss: Town Lattice
Length: 59 ft
Crosses: West Hill Brook
Location: Creamery Bridge
Rd, between West Hill Rd
and Hill West Rd, off North
Main St/Rt 118, Montgomery
GPS: 44.867688, -72.647989

Also known as Creamery
Bridge and Crystal Springs
Bridge. Remains of a
creamery are visible nearby.
Listed on the National
Register in 1974. Popular local swimming hole. Rough road, open
seasonally. Pedestrians should use care.

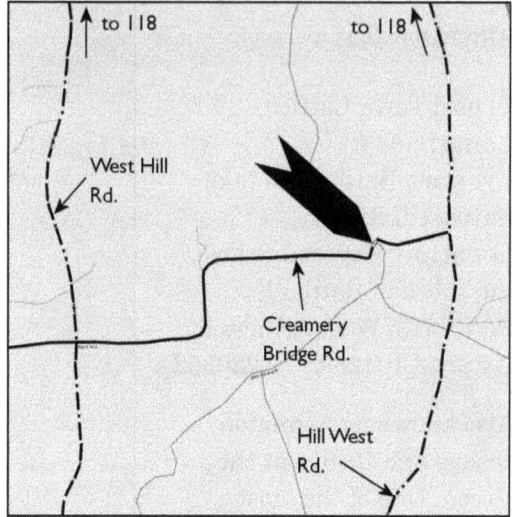

WILLARD BRIDGE (1870)

Truss: Town Lattice
Length: 123 ft
Crosses: Ottauquechee
River
Location: Mill St, off Rt 5 or
Evarts Rd, North Hartland
GPS: 43.593732, -72.349369

Also known as North
Hartland Bridge. This one is
the East bridge of twins (see
below). A cascading waterfall
is seen just downstream.
Listed on the National
Register in 1973. Open to vehicles.

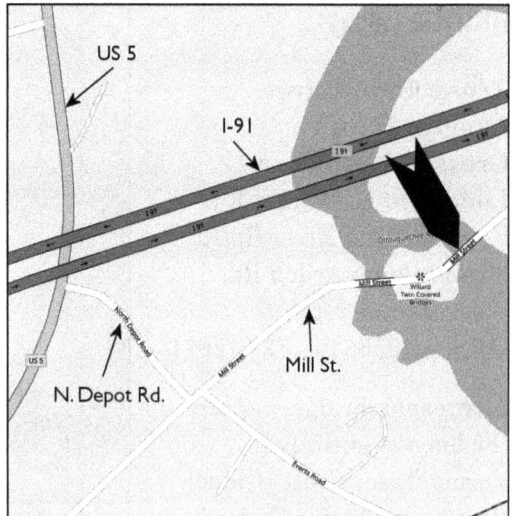

WILLARD TWIN BRIDGE (2001)

Truss: Town Lattice
Length: 80 ft
Crosses: Ottauquechee River
Location: Mill St, off Rt 5 or Evarts Rd, North Hartland
GPS: 43.593568, -72.350257

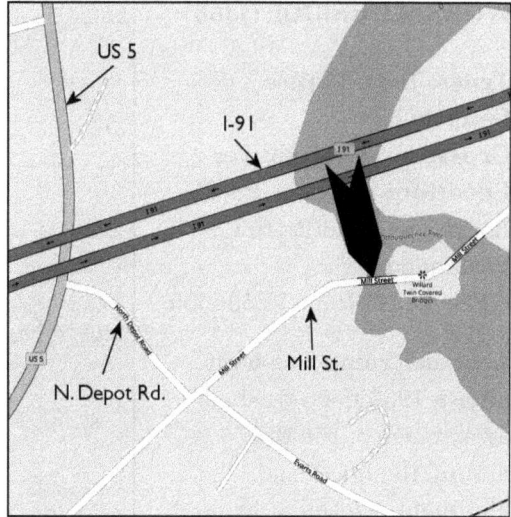

An earlier covered bridge was destroyed in a 1938 hurricane and replaced with a concrete bridge. Local support resulted in its replacement with a 19th-century style covered bridge in 2001. This one is the West twin. Open to vehicles.

WILLIAMSVILLE BRIDGE (1870)

Truss: Town Lattice
Length: 118 ft
Crosses: Rock River
Location: Dover Rd, Williamsville. Grimes Hill Rd, off Rt 30, Newfane becomes Dover Rd as does Dorr Fitch Rd, off Rt 100, Dover.
GPS: 42.942951, -72.686772

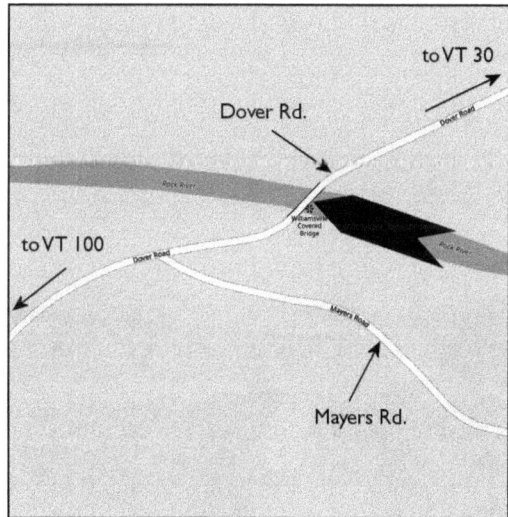

Listed on the National Register in 1973. Open to vehicles.

WORRALL BRIDGE (1868)

Truss: Town Lattice
Length: 82 ft
Crosses: Williams River
Location: Williams Rd of
Rockingham Rd/Rt 103,
Rockingham
GPS: 43.211783, -72.535605

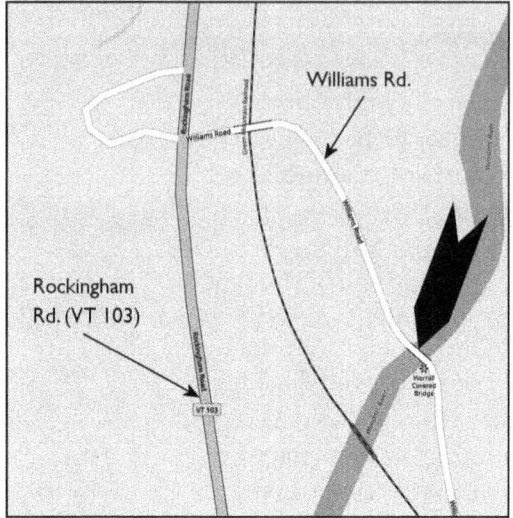

A wooden ramp was built
after a 1936 flood washed
away much of the soil
around the northeast
abutment. Closed after
damage in Hurricane Irene,
2011; reopened 2012. Listed on the National Register in 1973. Open to
vehicles.

CORNISH-WINDSOR BRIDGE • Windsor

VERMONT COVERED BRIDGE MUSEUM

The world's first museum dedicated to the history and preservation of covered bridges is closed as we go to press, due to the uncertain future of its host location.

Laumeister Art Center
44 Gypsy Lane, Bennington
GPS: 42.882451, -73.229548
Telephone (802) 442-7158

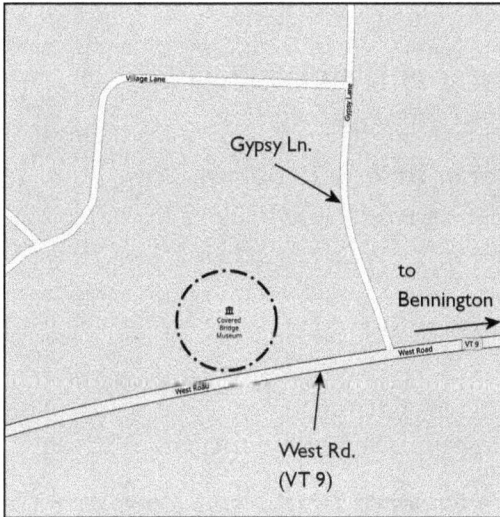

RESOURCES

ONLINE

Vermont Covered Bridge Society
vermontbridges.com

National Society for the Preservation of Covered Bridges
coveredbridgesociety.org

National Historic Covered Bridge Preservation Program
fhwa.dot.gov/bridge/covered.cfm

National Register of Historic Places
nps.gov/subjects/nationalregister

Vermont Historic Bridge Program
vtrans.vermont.gov/historic-bridges

BOOKS

Covered Bridges of Vermont
by Ed Barna, published by Countryman Press

New England's Covered Bridges: A Complete Guide
by Benjamin D. Evans and June R. Evans, published by
University Press of New England

Spanning Time: Vermont's Covered Bridges
by Joseph C. Nelson, published by New England Press

Vermont's Covered Bridges: A Guide for Explorers
by Harold Stiver, self-published

www.ingramcontent.com/pod-product-compliance
Lightning Source LLC
Chambersburg PA
CBHW070204060426
42445CB00032B/1180